ISRAEL'S GLORIOUS FUTURE

The Prophecies & Promises of God Revealed

Dr. Harold A. Sevener

IN THE U.S.:

CHOSEN PEOPLE MINISTRIES
241 East 51st Street
New York, NY 10022
212/223-2252

IN CANADA:

CHOSEN PEOPLE MINISTRIES (CANADA)
P.O. Box 897 Sta. B
North York, ON M2K 2R1
CANADA 416/250-0177

CPM

ISRAEL'S GLORIOUS FUTURE

TABLE OF CONTENTS

CHAPTER 3

PROLOGUE
BY HAROLD SEVENER

This book is written to celebrate the 3000 year anniversary of the city of Jerusalem, its glorious future as foretold by the biblical prophets, and to demonstrate the faithfulness of God in keeping His promises to the descendants of Abraham, Isaac and Jacob.

Israel's greatest prophet (apart from the Messiah), Moshe Rabbenu (Moses), uttered this great prophecy:

> When all these blessings and curses I have set before you come upon you and you take them to heart wherever the LORD your God disperses you among the nations, and when you and your children return to the LORD your God and obey him will all your heart and with all your soul according to everything I command you today, then the LORD your God will restore your fortunes and have compassion on you and gather you again from all the nations where he scattered you. Even if you have been banished to the most distant land under the heavens, from there the LORD your God will gather you and bring you back. He will bring you to the land that belonged to your fathers, and you will take possession of it. He will make you more prosperous and numerous than your fathers (Deuteronomy 30:1–5, NIV).

These amazing words were spoken by Moses to the people of Israel before they ever entered their promised land. Moses knew God was a "covenant-keeping" God. He had experienced God's faithfulness first-hand. He had played a leading role as God had unfolded the drama of Israel's miraculous deliverance from slavery in Egypt. He had witnessed God's preservation and protection of Israel during their forty years in the wilderness. He understood that Israel's failure to obey God would usher in a period of great persecution and calamity. However, Moses also knew that God would one day remember His promise to Abraham and would restore Israel to the land promised to them, where they would enjoy a glorious future which He had prepared for them.

Nearly 4000 years later, in fulfillment of prophecy, the children of Abraham, Isaac and Jacob again occupied the land promised to them by God. It would appear that God is preparing the stage of the Middle East to fulfill the promises of a Glorious Future for Israel.

Chapter 1
THE PROMISE FOR A GLORIOUS FUTURE

Israel is promised a glorious future by God Himself. God's promises and covenants are based solely upon His own sovereignty. It is the promises and covenants of God that distinguish Him from the gods of the pagans. One can measure God's character, justice, mercy and love through the promises He has made and fulfilled. He has never broken His Word to mankind or to Israel. His prophetic promises to Israel ensure their glorious future. The fulfillment of God's promises to Israel is an assurance to all who believe in Him that He will keep His promises to them.

ABRAHAM'S CONTRACT WITH GOD!

Middle Eastern culture embraced many ways of making (or in the Hebrew language, "cutting") enforceable contracts. Archaeological evidence demonstrates that in the days of Abraham ancient law distinguished between *bi-lateral* contracts (contracts where both parties agree to fulfill its terms) and *uni-lateral* contracts (contracts where only one party agrees to fulfill all of its terms). In theological terms, such contracts are called "*conditional*" (where both parties fulfill the terms) and "*unconditional*" (where only one party is called upon to fulfill the terms).

Scripture reveals that God entered into both types of contracts with Abram (Abraham). He entered into a bi-lateral contract when He called Abram to leave Ur of Chaldees (see Genesis 12:1–8). The blessing of Abram was contingent upon his leaving Ur. Once Abram left Ur of Chaldees, God was obligated to fulfill His part of the contract—to bless Abram and his seed, and to bless the people of earth through Abram's seed. Both parties fulfilled their part of the contract, and God has faithfully continued to fulfill His promise!

After Abram arrived in Canaan, God made another contract with him—a uni-lateral contract (unconditional covenant). The contract and the conditions under which it was made are stated in Genesis 15:1–21. The contract had two parts. The first part was God's promise to Abram that He would give him an heir. The second part was God's promise that He would give Abram land.

According to the biblical account, God declared to Abram that He would give to him and to his descendants a portion of real estate—from the river of Egypt (the Nile) to the river Euphrates. Having declared His intent to Abram, God asked Abram to gather the materials needed to "cut" the covenant. To execute the covenant, both parties were to pass between the gathered materials, but before Abram could fulfill his part of the covenant making process, God caused him to fall into a deep sleep. While Abram was asleep, God, Himself, passed between the materials, thus making a uni-lateral contract with Abram.

Abram, who was sleeping soundly, was powerless to fulfill any terms of the contract and, under Middle Eastern law, could not be held responsible for its fulfillment. Abram's sleep symbolized the fulfillment of the promise of an heir. Both Abram and Sarah were long past the age of bearing children. According to Scripture, their bodies were powerless to give birth (Hebrews 11:11–12; Romans 4:18–22). However, God had promised that Sarah would bear a son, an heir. In cutting a uni-lateral contract with Abram, God bore the sole responsibility of arranging conditions whereby that son could be born.

ABRAHAM SEEKS TO CHANGE
THE TERMS OF THE CONTRACT

God's timing is seldom man's timing. To Abram and Sarah, the long wait for God to fulfill the terms of the contract about their heir seemed endless. They took it upon themselves, therefore, to change the contract terms. Abram and Sarah agreed among themselves that Abram should have a child by Sarah's Egyptian handmaiden, Hagar. This child would be substituted for the child God had promised in His contract (see Genesis 16:1–16).

However, the plan that seemed so logical to Abram and Sarah did not meet with God's approval. God told Abram he could not alter the promises of the contract. The promises of a son through Sarah, and of a land, were fixed. The actions of Abram and Sarah now had to be accounted for in the prophetic program of God (see Genesis 16:5–14; 17:15–22; 18:11–15; 21:1–21). The seed of Abram through Sarah (Isaac) would inherit the land (maintaining title and dominion over the land), but because Ishmael was also Abram's son, the occupation of the land was now to be shared between the two brothers and their descendants (see Genesis 16:11–12; 21:11–13).

A PROPHET FROM AMONG THE PEOPLE

Famine in the land caused Abraham's descendants through Isaac and Jacob to journey to Egypt—a journey that resulted in their being held as slaves for 400 years (see Genesis 15:13–16). However, God remembered His promises to Abraham. He raised up the prophet Moses to deliver the children of Israel out of bondage.

Though unrecognized by the Israelites, God was their provider, their protector, their invisible King. He longed for the people to place their faith and trust in Him. He wanted the nation of Israel to demonstrate His grace and mercy to the other nations of the world.

God's plan for changing the children of Israel into a nation who trusted Him was astounding! He planned to dwell among the people of Israel (see Deuteronomy 12:4–7; 11:13–32). To execute his plan, He made a bi-lateral contract between Himself and the people. God agreed to dwell in the midst of the people and the people agreed to do all He asked (see Exodus 19:1–8). Considering the collective promise to Israel, God gave them the Law (Torah) (see Exodus 19–20). He also gave them the pattern for a Tabernacle (the portable structure where His Presence would dwell) which the people was to build according to the exact specifications given by God (see Exodus 25:8–40; 40:34–38).

God made it clear to Israel that their failure to keep the terms of the contract (obedience to God's commandments) would result in their being exiled from the land (see Deuteronomy 26:16–30:20). However, their ownership of the land, as promised to Abraham, Isaac and Jacob was not lost through disobedience and exile. Disobedience only affected the occupation of the land, and thus dominion over the land.

A KING ENTERS THE PICTURE

Once in the promised land, the children of Israel longed to have a king like the other nations. Ignoring the warnings of the prophet Samuel, they rejected God as their king and chose Saul to be king (see I Samuel 8:1–22). In choosing a king, the nation of Israel did not abrogate the contracts God had made with Abraham, either concerning the land or the blessing. Instead, God allowed another condition to be added. Just as God had incorporated the birth of Ishmael into the contracts with Abraham, He included the people's request for an earthly king to rule over them.

In allowing Israel to have an earthly king, God made one stipulation—that the offices of king and priest be kept separate (see 1 Samuel 10:8; 13:1–14; Zechariah 6:9–15). Saul forfeited the kingdom by disobeying that stipulation. God then gave the kingdom of Israel to David and to his descendants. In giving the kingdom to David, God included an additional promise. God promised that the house and lineage of David would have the throne of Israel forever. The throne and kingdom would never be taken away from them as it was from Saul and his descendants (See 2 Samuel 7:8–16).

THE LINES OF PROPHECY CONVERGE

Since God's program of redemption and judgment is fixed in eternity by His own sovereign decree, and since mankind was created with individual free-will, God, in His omniscience and foreknowledge, included the actions of mankind, both good and bad, to accomplish His prophetic program (see Acts 2:22–28).

In giving the promise of a king and a kingdom forever to the nation of Israel, God revealed how He would fulfill the prophecy and the promise He had made to Adam and Eve in the Garden of Eden. He promised He would provide a Redeemer through the seed of the woman to crush the head of Satan, thus putting an end to sin and restoring mankind to eternal fellowship with Himself (see Genesis 3:15).

In choosing Abraham, Isaac and Jacob, God chose the physical seed-line through which the Promised Redeemer (the Messiah) would come. In choosing a land, a place of sacrifice and worship, God chose how the prophecy of a Redeemer (Messiah) would be fulfilled. In giving to the lineage of David the promise of an everlasting kingdom, God demonstrated that He (through His Messiah) would always be the King of kings over Israel and the nations, and that one day Israel would have a glorious future in fulfillment of all He had promised.

To authenticate the promises and contracts (covenants) He had made with mankind, and with the seed of Abraham, Isaac and Jacob, in particular, God gave a written, inspired, infallible, trustworthy record of His promises, contracts, and dealings with mankind—the Holy Scriptures. The Scriptures, both the Old and the New Covenants (Testaments) are the objective proof of God's prophetic program in history. The annals of secular history and the spade of searching archaeologists continually verify the veracity of the Bible and of biblical prophecy.

Israel will have a glorious future because God has promised it; because He has contracted with Israel to make it happen!

Chapter 2
THE PREPARATION FOR A GLORIOUS FUTURE

Israel's glorious future is yet to come. While the kingdom of Israel under David and Solomon was expansive, the nation never reached or enjoyed the greatness of the kingdom as promised by God. The major factor leading to Israel's forfeiture of this blessing in the past was the people's sin, rebellion, unbelief and rejection of God.

Israel's rejection of God became apparent when they asked for an earthly king. Their rebellion and rejection of God culminated in their rejection of the Lord Jesus, God's Son manifest in the flesh. Jesus presented Himself as the Messiah, the son of David and rightful heir to the throne and kingdom of Israel. With the rejection of Jesus as Israel's earthly King and rightful heir to the throne of David, God's promise of judgment and dispersion came upon the nation of Israel. In 70 AD the city of Jerusalem and the Temple were destroyed by the armies of Titus, and the Jewish people were scattered among the nations of the world (the Diaspora).

Both biblical and secular history record the events that led to the dispersion of the kingdoms of Israel and Judah and to the destruction of the city of Jerusalem (the place where God had chosen to place His name) and its wondrous Temple (the place

7

where the Presence of God dwelt).

God forewarned Israel over and over again of pending judgment because of their unfaithfulness to Him. He warned that
they would lose their right to occupy the land, and their place of
blessing in the land, unless they repented of their sins. According to the contract of the Torah (the Law), Israel had agreed to
be obedient to all God asked and commanded of them. Through
the prophets, God admonished Israel that the kingdom they
longed for would be taken away from them and given to other
people (see Jeremiah 18:5–17; 25:8–14; Matthew 21:33–44). God
also specified the length of time the kingdom of Israel would
remain under Gentile control once Jerusalem was captured by
Nebuchadnezzar, King of Babylon. The prophet Jeremiah was
told the captivity would last for 70 years, and it did (see Jeremiah
25:8–14). However, because of the Israel's continual rejection
and rebellion against God during and after the 70 year captivity,
the prophet Daniel was told that the Gentile control over Israel
would last much longer (see Daniel 9:20–27).

A DIVINE TIMETABLE

Daniel was told that God had decreed "seventy-sevens" upon
the nation of Israel and upon the city of Jerusalem. During this
time God would ". . . finish transgression, to put an end to sin, to
atone for wickedness, to bring in everlasting righteousness, to
seal up vision and prophecy and to anoint the most holy" (Daniel
9:24, NIV).

The "seventy-sevens" are divided into three distinct prophetic groups representing a biblical year of 360 days. Two of
these prophetic groups of seven have been fulfilled historically.
Their fulfillment can be traced, not only in the Bible, but in
secular history as well. The first group of sevens designated a
period of time lasting 49 years (7x7). It began with a decree
issued by the Persian King Artaxerxes in the month of Nisan in
445 BC, which allowed the Jewish people to return from Babylon
and rebuild the walls of Jerusalem and their temple. The rebuild-

ing of the walls and the re-construction of the temple lasted until the month of Nisan in 396 BC. This part of the prophecy was fulfilled.

The second prophetic group of sevens lasted longer. Daniel was told that this designated period of time would cover 434 years (62x7) (see Daniel 9:26). At the end of this prophetic group of sevens, an "anointed one" (meaning the Messiah) would be "cut off" or "put to death." This second prophetic group of 62 sevens (434 years) began in the month Nisan 396 BC and lasted until the month Nisan in 33 AD.

According to the Scriptures and secular history, 33 AD was the year in which the Lord Jesus, the Messiah of Israel, the promised Redeemer, the Son of God, was crucified. The apostle Luke states that Jesus began His ministry in the 15th year of Tiberias Caesar (see Luke 3:1). Scripture also reveals that Jesus kept four Passovers. These Scriptural facts confirm that the promised Messiah was cut off on April 6, 33 AD.

The last group of prophetic sevens, according to Daniel, contain only one seven year period (see Daniel 9:27). It can be distinguished from the others by the fact that it will be divided into two parts. According to Daniel, in the middle of this last seven year period (or after 3-1/2 years), a covenant that was confirmed between Israel and the ruling prince of the nations will be broken. Daniel was also told this same prince will stop all sacrifices in the temple, causing great desolation to the temple and the city of Jerusalem. Daniel was then told that the prince will "place abominations on the wing of [the temple] until the time of the end (see Daniel 9:27).

Various attempts have been made to fit the events of this last period of prophetic sevens into the history of Israel, but all such attempts have failed. These events are still in Israel's future! The description of events that take place during this last seven year period did not happen when Titus destroyed the Temple in 70 AD. They also do not fit the events of the Bar Kochba rebellions in 133–135 AD. The events described in this last seven year period fit into a time Jesus and John called the Tribulation or Great Tribulation (see Matthew 24:1–35; Revelation 6–19)—a time in Israel's prophetic future.

Once the temple was destroyed and the city of Jerusalem came under the control of the Gentile nations, this last prophetic seven year period remained unfulfilled. If the events of this seven year period remain unfulfilled, the promises and prophecies concerning Israel's glorious future could never happen. Israel could never have a glorious future and God's promises would be invalidated. However, since God cannot break His word, and since He keeps all of the contracts (covenants) and promises He has ever made, this last seven year period in Israel's prophetic future will take place! Then, and only then, will Israel enjoy the glorious future kingdom God has prepared for them.

RETURNING TO THE LAND

Before the events of the last seven year period (the Tribulation), as prophesied by Daniel, can be fulfilled, Israel must exist as a nation; they must control the city of Jerusalem; they must have the opportunity and the time to rebuild the Temple. It would be impossible for Israel to accomplish these things during the seven year Tribulation as described by the prophets. There would neither be time nor opportunity. During the Tribulation, Israel will undergo great persecution. They will be fighting to survive. The prophet Jeremiah calls this period in Israel's future "the time of Jacob's Trouble" (see Jeremiah 30:7). There will be no building projects. Instead, there will be mass destruction of buildings and properties in Israel and throughout the world.

According to Daniel's prophecy, the last seven years (the Tribulation) begins with the confirmation of a covenant between Israel and the prince of the nations (see Daniel 9:27). This can only happen if the nation of Israel is established and in control of the city of Jerusalem prior to the commencement of the Tribulation.

A RETURN IN UNBELIEF

God's prophetic program for Israel began with the signing of a covenant—between Himself and Abraham. The Tribulation will also begin with the signing of a covenant—between Israel and the leader of the Gentile nations. The signing of such a covenant implies that the Jewish people who return to the land prior to the commencement of the Tribulation will not be a nation trusting in the God of Abraham, Isaac and Jacob. Instead, they will be a nation trusting in their own religion, with their own political agenda. They will be trusting in the strength of men and nations rather than in God.

This is exactly the way the prophet Ezekiel foresaw the return of the Jewish people in the latter days (or in the days before the Tribulation begins). Ezekiel prophesied:

> Therefore say to the house of Israel, "This is what the Sovereign LORD says: It is not for your sake, O house of Israel, that I am going to do these things, but for the sake of my holy name, which you have profaned among the nations where you have gone. I will show the holiness of my great name, which has been profaned among the nations, the name you have profaned among them. Then the nations will know that I am the LORD, declares the Sovereign LORD, when I show myself holy through you before their eyes. For I will take you out of the nations; I will gather you from all the countries and bring you back into your own land" (Ezekiel 36:22–24, NIV).

The prophet Ezekiel says God will bring the Jewish people back into the land of Israel for the sake of His holy name. Since God made contracts (covenants) with the nation of Israel, and because He keeps His promises, He must bring the Jewish people back to the land promised to the descendants of Isaac—whether they are trusting in Him or not. In fact, the prophet emphasizes that God will bring them back even though they profane His holy name. God will not break His word. He will not break His covenants!

Notice the language of this prophecy implies both a world-wide dispersion of the Jewish people and a world-wide re-gathering of the Jewish people to the land of Israel.

This prophecy cannot apply to the return of the Jewish people from Babylon after the 70 year captivity. According to Scripture, only 42,360 Jews returned from Babylon. There is no mention of Jewish people returning from other countries (see Ezra 2:64).

The only time in Israel's history when there has been a world-wide re-gathering of the Jewish people to the land of Israel was the period from the beginning of this century to the present. Israel's population continues to increase while the Jewish population among the countries of the world where they have lived for centuries is declining.

Interestingly, the return of the Jewish people in this century is marked by the political and religious agenda of Zionism, rather than by a deep-rooted faith in the promises of God, His Word, in the Messiah, or an interest in rebuilding the Temple. In contrast, the remnant of Jewish people returning from Babylon had a desire to serve God, to rebuild Jerusalem and the Temple so that God would return to His house and to His people. It would appear that the words of the prophet Ezekiel apply directly to the Jewish people and the nation of Israel as they exist today. God is bringing them back because He keeps His promises!

RECLAIMING LAND AND REBUILDING RUINED CITIES

The prophet Ezekiel not only prophesied that God would bring the Jewish people back into their land, regardless of whether or not they trusted in Him, he also said God would prepare the soil of the land of Israel in anticipation of their return (see Ezekiel 36:8–12). This did not happen when the Jewish people returned from Babylon. Instead, within a few short years the continuous fighting and conquests caused the land to become increasingly barren.

After the destruction of Jerusalem in 70 AD, and the subsequent conflicts with Jewish zealots, the Romans devastated the land. Under Christian, Muslim, Turkish and British rule, the land became almost totally devoid of flora and fauna. Through the centuries the desert sands encroached upon once-inhabited areas of the land. Conquering nations were unable to restore the land to its former state of productivity and beauty.

Then came the return of the Jewish people! In fulfillment of His promises, God had prepared the land. Today, the State of Israel is truly a modern day miracle!

When the first Jewish pioneers began to trickle back to the land during the latter half of the 1800's, they encountered malaria-filled swamps, barren mountains and ruined terraces where once lush gardens had grown. The land was hostile and did not seem fit for habitation. The task of reclaiming the land seemed impossible, and claimed many lives.

Not only did the early Jewish settlers face a hostile land, they were threatened on every side by hostile neighbors within the land. As war raged in Europe, resulting in the agonizing deaths of 6,000,000 Jewish people, and in the suffering of millions more as they endured the brutality thrust upon them in the concentration camps of Europe, the Jewish pioneers toiled to rebuild a homeland for the Jewish people—clearing the land, rebuilding cities, restoring the crops and plant life that had once flourished in the land.

By the time Israel was declared a nation in 1948, the reforestation projects had made an impact on both the look of the land and on the ecology. The swamps that had been drained were producing crops for the people of Israel. Today, the land of Israel produces crops for export all over the world. The once-barren Negev is alive with people inhabiting new cities where ancient cities once stood. Farming and industry flourish, pumping millions of dollars into the Israeli economy. The prophet Isaiah said, "the desert (Negev) will blossom like a rose" (see Isaiah 35:1), and it has!

Once again, it is emphasized that this century is the only time these prophetic events have happened in Israel's history.

THE DRY BONES THAT BECAME AN ARMY

The prophet Ezekiel not only prophesied the return of the people in unbelief, the reclamation of the land, the rebuilding of the cities, and the reforestation of the mountains of Israel, he also prophesied that when Israel did return to the land they would be a great army of people (see Ezekiel 37:10).

The prophecy of the "Dry Bones" of Ezekiel 37 is perhaps one of the best known of all the prophecies in the Bible. It is a visual picture of the restoration of Israel. The nation is pictured as dry bones—devoid of life and disjointed. The prophet watched as God caused skin, tendons and flesh to come upon the bones. The prophet was commanded to "prophesy to them," and when he did the "four winds from heaven" breathed life into them and they became a vast army of people. The prophet is then told, "Therefore prophesy and say to them: 'This is what the Sovereign LORD says: O my people, I am going to open your graves and bring you up from them; I will bring you back to the land of Israel'" (Ezekiel 37:12, NIV).

When Yigael Yadin was excavating Masada his team uncovered a building thought to be a synagogue. As they excavated further, the Genizah (hiding) was found. The Genizah is the hiding place for sacred scrolls that are no longer fit for use. To the team's absolute amazement, they found a fragment of scroll. When the text was deciphered they were even more amazed, and sobered. The fragment was an ancient Hebrew text of Ezekiel 37. Finding this prophecy at Masada, buried under centuries of dust and debris, confirmed to many on the team, and to many Israelis in general, that the modern state of Israel is a fulfillment of Ezekiel's vision of the dry bones.

Further evidence to support the fact that Ezekiel 37 is being fulfilled by the modern state of Israel in this century, is the use of the phrase "vast army" or "exceeding great army" (v.9). Because of the political unrest in the Middle East, Israel has remained in a state of war with the Arab world since its founding in 1948. Every Israeli citizen (male and female) must serve in the army. Israel has one of the most efficient, effective armies in the world today. Even with the recent peace agreements with Egypt, Jordan and the Palestinians, Israel still must maintain its "exceeding great army," lest it be over-powered by its enemies.

AN INVASION THAT TRIGGERS THE END

The prophet Ezekiel gave an additional prophecy concerning Israel and the events that lead to the Tribulation and to the completion of Daniel's vision of the final seven years. He states:

> *After many days you will be summoned; in the latter years you will come into the land that is restored from the sword, whose inhabitants have been gathered from many nations to the mountains of Israel which had been a continual waste; but its people were brought out from the nations, and they are living securely, all of them (Ezekiel 38:8, NASV).*

At first glance, it appears that this prophecy is a summarization of what Ezekiel had prophesied previously about the nation of Israel. However, upon closer examination, it appears that Ezekiel is foretelling the actual conditions under which Israel will exist prior to the events of the Tribulation. He does so by warning Israel that their land will be invaded by a nation from the north which has joined forces with a coalition of nations surrounding the land of Israel (see Ezekiel 38–39).

Until this century, the conditions under which Israel will exist as a nation prior to this invasion had never been met in Israel's history. Notice what these conditions are, and notice how precisely they have been fulfilled by the modern State of Israel.

WARFARE

The prophet states that the invasion from the north will

take place after the following events have come to pass:

After the land of Israel has been restored from the sword (Ezekiel 38:8). Literally, this means that the northern invasion of Israel cannot take place until Israel gains its land through warfare (the sword) and has been victorious sufficiently to negotiate peace.

The only time that this has happened in Israel's history was during the latter half of this century. Israel gained its land through warfare and has maintained its land by warfare. It must be said that it was not the intent of the Israelis to provoke their Arab neighbors to war. In 1947, the Jewish settlers were willing to accept the United Nations plan to "partition Palestine." However, the Arab world was not willing to accept such a partition. In 1948, when Israel was declared a state and the nation of Israel was born, the Arab world immediately attacked.

Unable to destroy the nation of Israel through armed conflict, the Arab world sought to destroy Israel through economic boycott. The Arab world refused to do business with any company doing business with the Jewish state of Israel. Unsuccessful in their boycotts of Israel, the Arab world then sought Israel's destruction through the United Nations—seeking to equate Zionism with racism and seeking to isolate the Jewish state from its western allies.

Unsuccessful in their attempts to destroy Israel, the Arab world turned to a propaganda war, a media war, pitting the Israeli army against the helpless Palestinian people. The media soon portrayed Israel as a mighty Goliath of the Middle East bullying a tiny David, the Palestinian people. Photos of Israeli soldiers armed with machine guns, tanks, and the latest military hardware accompanied front-page news articles. More often than not, photos of the Palestinians, by contrast, were of individuals (often children) being beaten and mercilessly gunned down by the cruel, but effective Israeli army.

Still unsuccessful in their attempts to destroy Israel, one of the Arab countries, Iraq, invaded Kuwait in an attempt to bring Israel into armed conflict with a united Arab world. Despite the casualties and loss of life caused by Iraqi missiles falling on Tel Aviv and on other parts of the county, Israel did not retaliate. Following the advice of its Western allies, Israel remained neutral.

Despite criticism and propaganda, Israel never wavered. From their position of strength, they continued to negotiate for peace with their Arab neighbors. Their persistence has been rewarded. Egypt was the first to make peace, but the price was high—the death of President Anwar Sadat. In 1994–95, peace agreements were signed between Israel and the Palestinians, then between Israel and Jordan. Once again, the price was high—the death of the Israeli Prime Minister, Yitzhak Rabin. Even now, Israel is negotiating a peace treaty with Syria and it appears that one will be signed!

As stated, the Tribulation begins with the confirmation of a covenant (contract) between Israel and the prince of the nations (see Daniel 9:26, 27). This means the prince of the nations (who is later identified as anti-Christ) will enforce an existing covenant that Israel has made. One cannot help wonder if the covenants (peace agreements) Israel is now signing will be the basis for the final peace agreement that will trigger the Tribulation. Both Daniel and the Revelation indicate that the Tribulation will begin with an era of peace, but that the peace will be shattered when the anti-Christ unveils his diabolical plan to destroy Israel.

AN INCREASING POPULATION

Not only does the prophet Ezekiel state that the northern invasion of Israel will take place after Israel has gained and maintained its land through warfare and is at peace, he further states that:

The invasion will take place after Israel has been gathered from many nations (see Ezekiel 38:8). As already seen, Ezekiel prophesied that God would re-gather Israel and would bring them into their own land. He re-emphasizes the re-gathering as a fulfilled condition of what must take place before the northern nation can invade, and as a fulfilled condition before the Tribulation can begin. Today there are more Jews living in Israel than in any one single country of the world. Until recently, the largest concentration of Jewish people was in the United States, followed by the former Soviet Union. With a declining birth rate among the Jewish population in the Diaspora, and with increasing numbers of Soviet and East European Jews immigrating to Israel, the Jewish population of Israel has increased to over 6,000,000. This means nearly 50% of the 13,000,000 Jews living in the world are now living in Israel.

Once again it should be noted there has never before been such a large re-gathering of the Jewish people in Israel's history. When the Assyrians took the northern tribes of Israel captive in 721 BC, a small number returned to the land but the majority remained in captivity. When the Babylonians took the southern tribes of Israel into captivity (606 BC to 586 BC) only a small remnant returned. The greater numbers of Jewish people remained in the expansive Babylonian, Persian, Grecian, Egyptian and Roman empires.

From the time of the Roman conquest of Israel to the time of the signing of the Balfour Declaration in 1917, only small remnants of Jewish people had returned to live in the land of Israel. However, from 1917 to the present day, the Jewish population of Israel has exploded—exactly fulfilling Ezekiel's prophecy of the last days!

MOUNTAINS NO LONGER WASTE

To ensure that there be no misunderstanding about the period of time he was describing, the prophet repeats three additional conditions to be met by Israel before the northern invasion can happen and the seven year Tribulation begin. He states:

It will take place after the mountains of Israel have been reforested (see Ezekiel 38:8). Notice the use of the past tense in this verse. The prophet states: ". . . to the mountains of Israel which had been a continual waste" (NASV). In using the past tense, the prophet directly implies that the mountains are no longer a waste. Unless God miraculously intervenes, changing mountains requires time! But, as has been noted, the early Jewish settlers quickly recognized the importance of restoring the flora and fauna of the land. They therefore established a systematic program of reforestation of the mountains. To date, the Jewish National Fund has planted millions of trees throughout the land. Trees are planted in memory of loved ones, in honor of special occasions, and by tourists visiting the land. Any and every occasion is seized for planting and reforesting the mountains.

Not only have trees been planted on the mountains of Israel, but vineyards have also been planted. Ancient terraces have been restored, and new terracing has been built so the mountainsides can be cultivated. The words of Ezekiel, "O mountains of Israel, you will put forth your branches and bear your fruit for My people Israel" (see Ezekiel 36:8, NASV) have been fulfilled in our days!

A NATION WITHIN NATIONS

A second condition of the end time events given by Ezekiel is the fact that *Israel will exist as a multi-ethnic nation.* He says: ". . . but its people were brought out from the nations" (Ezekiel 38:8, NASV). The phrase "its people" is not in the Hebrew text. This phrase was added by translators. Leaving the phrase "its people" out of the verse implies that the nation of Israel was brought out from the nations, or that the nations were responsible for the establishment of Israel. If this is the correct meaning of this text, it is certainly another confirmation that the modern state of Israel is the fulfillment of Ezekiel's prophecy. Israel was established by a vote of the United Nations. The Gentile nations of the world voted unanimously to establish a national homeland for the Jewish people. The only other time in Israel's history when a similar event took place was when Cyrus, the king of Persia, made a decree which set the stage for the

return of the Jews from Babylon (Isaiah 44:28)—an event which
set in motion the prophetic events that ultimately led to the
birth of the Messiah, the Lord Jesus and to the unveiling of God's
program of redemption for Jews and Gentiles alike through the
death, burial and resurrection of Jesus.

While this translation of the verse certainly shows fulfillment in the modern State of Israel, so does the translation that
includes the phrase "its people." If this is what the prophet meant
to say, one could understand the verse to mean that the people
of Israel, brought forth out of the nations, would themselves be
distinct. That is, there would be ethnic distinction among the
citizens of modern Israel.

This, of course, is exactly what one finds in Israel today. Its
citizenship comprises people from all nations, not just Jews. Some
of Israel's citizens are identified by their country of origin, others
are identified by their religious faith. Currently, Israel is faced
with an even greater challenge among its citizenship—a Palestinian state within its borders. A nation within a nation!

Once again, one is reminded that this is the only time in
Israel's history when its citizenship has been multi-national, to
the point of having another nation living within its borders.

DWELLING CONFIDENTLY IN THE LAND

Ezekiel adds one last condition to show how Israel will
be dwelling in their land before the northern invasion, and
before the Tribulation begins. He says the people of Israel will
be ". . .living securely, all of them" (Ezekiel 38:8, NASV). The
word translated "securely" could also be translated "confidently."
Either translation fits with the conditions under which the modern State of Israel exists. Their security and confidence stem
from their military strength and political strategy.

In their quest for peace with their Arab neighbors, the leaders of Israel have determined a policy of trading land for peace.
This is not a popular policy among some Israelis and Arabs, especially among some of the religious Jews and Arabs. In fact,

this policy has caused bitter division among some groups of Israeli and Arab citizens, and may yet lead to more internal violence in the land. But the policy is in effect nonetheless, and land is being surrendered as peace agreements are being signed.

The only way such a policy could be made and maintained is from a position of strength, confidence and security; otherwise, it would be certain suicide. Perhaps this is why the prophet includes the reference to "confidence" and "security" at this point in his prophecy.

He has already indicated that Israel will return to the land not trusting in the God of Abraham, Isaac and Jacob, but trusting in their own strength and in man-made covenants and alliances.

THE SEED OF ISHMAEL AND ESAU

It should not go unnoticed that the prophet Ezekiel includes the descendants of Ishmael and Esau (Arabs and Palestinians) in his prophecy concerning Israeli return to the land. God's promises and covenants with Abraham and Hagar extended the right of occupancy in the land to the descendants of Ishmael and of Esau, as well as to the descendants of Isaac. However, the right to occupy the land was contingent upon obedience to the God of Abraham.

Just as God warned Israel that disobedience and rebellion against Him would result in dispersion from the land, He warned the descendants of Ishmael and Esau that disobedience and rebellion, especially in their treatment of Israel, would bring certain and swift judgment (see Isaiah 21:1–17). But His judgment upon the Arab world would not be dispersion from the land (as He had warned Israel). Instead, His judgment upon the descendants of Ishmael and Esau would be devastation and desolation of the land. Ezekiel prophesied:

Son of man, set your face against Mount Seir [Edom], *and prophesy against it, and say to it, "Thus says the Lord GOD, 'Behold, I am against you, Mount Seir,*

And I will stretch out My hand against you,
And I will make you a desolation and a waste.
I will lay waste your cities,
And you will become a desolation.
Then you will know that I am the LORD.
Because you have had everlasting enmity and have deliv-
ered the sons of Israel to the power of the sword at the time
of their calamity, at the time of the punishment of the end'"
. . . "I will make you an everlasting desolation, and your
cities will not be inhabited. Then you will know that I am
the LORD. Because you have said, 'These two nations
[Judah & Israel] and these two lands will be mine, and we
will possess them,' although the LORD was there, there-
fore, as I live," declares the Lord GOD, "I will deal with
you according to your anger and according to your envy
which you showed because of your hatred against them; so
I will make Myself known among them when I judge you"
(Ezekiel 35:2–11, NASV).

This amazing prophecy about the Arab world has past,
present and future application. Because the descendants of
Ishmael and Esau failed to accept the contract (covenant) and
promises which God had extended through Isaac and Jacob, and
because they joined forces with surrounding Gentile nations seeking Israel's destruction, they came under the judgment of God.
The promises and judgments visited upon the descendants of
Abraham through Isaac and Ishmael, were reciprocal. If God
blessed Israel, the Arab world received blessing. If God judged
Israel, the Arab world received judgment.

As descendants of Isaac, Israel received title to the land,
and thus dominion over the land. But privilege brings responsibility. Israel had the greater responsibility of demonstrating God's
love and grace to the descendants of Ishmael and Esau. They
were accountable for living righteous lives so that God's blessing in the land would continue. God had made it clear that Israel's

dispersion from the land would bring devastation to the land and hardship and judgment to the Arab world. So important was this reciprocal relationship within the promises of God, that He commanded Israel not to hate the descendants of Esau (which would include Ishmael's seed), and the Egyptians. They were to be welcomed into the camp of Israel. God said:

> You shall not detest [hate] an Edomite, for he is your brother; you shall not detest [hate] an Egyptian, because you were an alien in his land. The sons of the third generation who are born to them may enter the assembly of the LORD (Deuteronomy 23:7–8, NASV).

Israel failed to be obedient to God. They failed in their commission to be "a light unto the nations." The Arab world, deprived of God's truth, became envious of Israel's position among the nations and fell easy prey to satanic deception. They joined forces with the surrounding Gentile nations and empires seeking Israel's destruction.

Not having a knowledge of the promises of God, the Arab world still does not understand that when they seek Israel's destruction they bring God's judgment upon themselves. They do not understand that they should seek Israel's good so that they, too, will find God's goodness extended to them.

After the destruction of the Temple in 70 AD and the dispersion of the Jewish people among the nations, the land of Israel became increasingly desolate. The Arab people living in the land have suffered, just as God promised.

THE RISE OF ISLAM

As desolation engulfed the land, poverty fell upon the inhabitants of the land. The spiritual bankruptcy within Judaism and organized Christianity created a spiritual vacuum that swept over the Middle East.

In 611 AD, recognizing this void, a descendent of Ishmael

and Esau named Mohammed claimed to have a new revelation from God. By 622 AD, Mohammed had gained a large following to his new religion [Islam-Moslem], and he and his disciples waged a holy war [*hejira*] against the city of Medina. Two years later, in 624 AD, they waged a holy war on Mecca and captured the city. Within a few years, Mohammed and his followers were able to capture and convert to Islam the entire Arabian peninsula. By the end of the 11th century AD, Mohammed and his band of followers had captured all of the Middle East, northern Africa, and parts of Europe, including Spain, making Islam the religion of those areas. As the religion of Islam spread, so did the Arabic language and culture.

Islam was filling the spiritual void created by the failed attempts of Judaism and organized Christianity. The Koran (Islam's sacred writings) was written with Ishmael's name replacing the names of Isaac and Jacob where Scripture records God's promises to Isaac and Jacob. Had Mohammed and his followers known the Scriptures better, they would have known of God's promise that the descendants of Ishmael and of Esau would become a great and powerful nation (see Genesis 16:7–16; 17:20; 21:12–21). It was not necessary to re-write God's promises. In fact, God warned against their seeking to take possession of the land of Israel, the city of Jerusalem, and the Temple (see Ezekiel 35:10–11), saying that such action would bring upon them a greater judgment of God (see Ezekiel 35:11–15).

It should be noted that during its rise to power, the Arab world lived to the east of the nation of Israel, just as God said they would (see Genesis 16:12, NASV). God does keep his promises!

In 637 AD, the Moslems conquered Jerusalem, and by 691 AD Caliph Abd al-Malik had completed building the Dome of the Rock—a large Islamic mosque built over the site he believed was the original Temple site. Abd al-Malik claimed it was the place where Abraham attempted to sacrifice "Ishmael" (according to the Koran). He also claimed that it was the place where

Mohammed ascended into heaven upon his white horse. Later it was declared that the rock, over which the Dome was built, covered the door of the place where the souls of all men are kept. These declarations made Jerusalem, which is never mentioned in the Koran, the third most sacred city to the Moslem world. The first is Mecca and the second Medina.

But the capture of the city of Jerusalem was the beginning of the end for the glorious Moslem empire in the Middle East. Their empire continued to increase in strength and power everywhere *except* in the Middle East. Just as God had promised, the land and cities became desolate. Wars and conflicts ravaged the land, leaving its people destitute and its farmland barren.

Moslem control of the city of Jerusalem enraged both the Christian world and Jewish world. Neither could believe that God would allow such a thing to happen! The Jews could do little; they were a people without a country, and were subject to strict laws governing their lives as they lived among the citizens of the Gentile world. A few did what they could to try to regain the land, others simply prayed for the Messiah to come and deliver them.

The Christian world was in a better position, or so they thought! From 1099 through 1187 AD, the leaders of Europe and Britain organized crusades to liberate the Holy land from the infidels. But in their quest to conquer the land of Israel for Christianity, the Crusaders only further ravished it. Although they were successful in their capture of Jerusalem for Christianity, they could not continue their conquests. In 1187 AD, Saladin recaptured Jerusalem, putting an end to the Crusader control of the city and of the land of Israel.

From 1187 AD to the beginning of this century (c.1900), except for the year 1537 AD when Sultan Suleiman the Magnificent embellished the Dome of the Rock and built huge walls around the city of Jerusalem, the city and the land continued to become more desolate. Concurrently, the power and prestige of the Arab world declined.

In 1917 the British conquered Jerusalem and the Arab world

was divided into lands and kingdoms as determined by Britain and the Western powers.

Israel's re-birth and the momentum of its rapid growth as a recognized nation and world power created opportunities for the Arab world to also gain in strength and power. The world's need for oil transformed the Arab countries from poverty-stricken backward areas into a league of nations now among the wealthiest and best equipped military powers in the world.

As the Arab world has increased in its sphere of power and prestige, the right-wing extremists within Islam have strengthened their sphere, fostering hatred toward the modern nation of Israel. They are militant in their determination to see that no peace process with Israel will ever be successful. They are determined to destroy the nation of Israel. They do not understand that in God's prophetic program their actions will lead to their own destruction.

THE NORTHERN INVASION OF ISRAEL

Ezekiel lists the countries who will invade Israel, and thus usher in the Tribulation. He states: "Persia, Ethiopia, and Put with them, all of them *with* shield and helmet; Gomer with all its troops; Beth-togarmah *from* the remote parts of the north with all its troops—many peoples with you" (Ezekiel 38:5–6, NASV).

Persia is now identified as the modern country of Iran. Ethiopia is identified as itself. *Put* (*Cush*) is identified with modern Libya and the North African nations. Gomer represents the modern nation of Syria. *Beth Togarmah* symbolizes the countries further north of Israel—Turkey and probably Southern Russia and her allies. Interestingly, the principal religion today in each of these countries is Islam. Today, news reports frequently broadcast stories of the open conflict that exists between the militant Islamic fundamentalists who call for a holy war on Israel and its supporting allies, and the more moderate Moslems who seek peace.

The prophet Ezekiel also prophesied of a larger involvement

of nations called *Gog* of the land of *Magog*, led by the prince of *Rosh* (or as the Hebrew suggests, the "chief prince of Meshech and Tubal") (see Ezekiel 38:1–2, NASV).

The word "Rosh," as it appears in many English translations, comes from a transliteration of the Hebrew word "Rosh" (meaning chief) into "Ros" in the Greek Septuagint translation of the Hebrew Scriptures (c. 3rd. century BC).

As to why the Jewish scribes would transliterate the Hebrew word "Rosh" into Greek, in the form of a proper name for a country or nation, is not clear. Perhaps a clue lies in the fact that at the time of the Septuagint translation there was a warlike tribe of people, called the Scythians, who occupied the far recesses of the north. The ancient rabbis believed the Scythians represented the forces of evil led by Satan himself. They identified the Scythians as *Rosh*, of the land of Gog and Magog, who would invade Israel in the latter days.

While the ancient rabbis believed *Rosh* represented the Scythians, they also believed that Gog and the land of Magog were a derivative of the Sumerian word "Gug," meaning "darkness." Magog was the "land of darkness." Thus, Gog and Magog assumed the role of the personification of all that is darkness and evil within a nation.

Within rabbinic literature, and within Scripture, Gog and Magog and the Chief Prince of *Meshech* and *Tubal* became a title applied to evil and dark nations which were led by the forces of evil, seeking the destruction of Israel. They are nations that have come under satanic control. John uses the title of Gog and Magog to describe the nations at the end of the 1,000 year Kingdom Age that, under Satan's leadership, seek the destruction of the people of God (see Revelation 20:7–8).

This is exactly the way the prophet Ezekiel uses Gog and Magog. He uses it as a symbolic title for the nations of the world that will seek Israel's destruction once they have been re-gathered to their land. It is a comprehensive vision of satanic hatred, manifested as greed and envy, as the nations of the world join forces with the nations surrounding Israel (see Ezekiel 38:11–12).

The Psalmist envisioned this conspiracy of nations coming against Israel when he wrote:

> O God, do not remain quiet;
> Do not be silent and, O God, do not be still.
> For, behold, Thine enemies make an uproar;
> And those who hate Thee have exalted themselves.
> They make shrewd plans against Thy people,
> And conspire together against Thy treasured ones.
> They have said, "Come, and let us wipe them out as a nation;
> That the name of Israel be remembered no more."
> For they have conspired together with one mind;
> Against Thee do they make a covenant:
> The tents of Edom and the Ishmaelites;
> Moab, and the Hagarites;
> Gebal, and Ammon, and Amalek;
> Philistia with the inhabitants of Tyre;
> Assyria also has joined with them;
> They have become a help to the children of Lot [Selah]
> (Psalm 83:1–8, NASV).

Notice that the Arab nations mentioned by the Psalmist include the descendants of Ishmael and of Edom. Their descendants are the very people with whom Israel is presently making covenants of peace. It would appear that the present peace process will come to a sudden end as the battle of Gog and Magog puts into motion the final events of God's prophetic program for the Tribulation itself.

THE DESTRUCTION OF GOG AND MAGOG

The prophet Isaiah said of Israel, "No weapon that is formed against you shall prosper. . . " (Isaiah 54:17, NASV). Gog and Magog, invading Israel from the north, and the surrounding Arab nations invading from the south and east will discover the truth of this prophecy too late. According to Ezekiel's prophecy, the armies of Gog and Magog, along with the Arab alliance, will be destroyed upon the mountains of Israel (see Ezekiel 39:1–20).

How complete will the destruction be? What form will this destruction take? Scripture is not specific, leaving the answers open to interpretation. Ezekiel states, however, that God will send fire upon Gog and Magog (Ezekiel 39:6). He says their troops will fall upon the mountains of Israel and become food for predatory birds (Ezekiel 39:4). The prophet Malachi indicates that the cities and the land reclaimed by the descendants of Ishmael and Edom (this reclamation is currently going on in Israel because of the signed peace treaties) will also be destroyed (see Malachi 1:2–5).

One's interpretation of how complete the destruction of Gog and Magog will be is determined, in part, by their understanding of when (in God's prophetic program) the battle will take place. A puzzling problem in trying to identify the time frame of the battle of Gog and Magog is Ezekiel's description of the aftermath of the battle. He states that it will take seven months to bury the dead (see Ezekiel 39:11–16). He also indicates that Israel will burn the captured weapons of Gog and Magog for seven years (see Ezekiel 39:9–10). Bible scholars who believe the battle of Gog and Magog will take place at the end of the Tribulation teach that Israel will bury the dead, cleanse the land and burn the weapons either prior to the beginning, or during the first part, of the Kingdom

Other Bible scholars place the battle of Gog and Magog toward the middle of Tribulation. Still others believe the battle of Gog and Magog will take place before the Tribulation begins, thus setting into motion the events that cause the Tribulation. The latter view best fits the context of Ezekiel's prophecy.

According to this view, Gog and Magog could invade the land of Israel at least three and one half years before the Tribulation begins, or as much as seven years before the Tribulation begins. Since the Tribulation begins with an era of peace which will last approximately three and one half years before the peace "covenant" is broken by the anti-Christ, the invasion by Gog and Magog could take place three and one half years prior to the beginning of the Tribulation, thus allowing for the seven year period for burning the weapons and meeting the conditions of peace as prophesied by Ezekiel. Or, it could take place a full seven years before the Tribulation begins, thus giving some ten and one half years of peace to set into motion the events of the Tribulation.

While one cannot be certain, it does seem that the destruction of Gog and Magog fits into God's prophetic program as an event prior to the Tribulation rather than as an event within the Tribulation, or just prior to or within the Kingdom.

If this is the case, it would appear that events taking place in the Middle East today are a dramatic fulfillment of Ezekiel prophecy. As peace treaties are signed, and as economic stability comes to the Middle East, nations and peoples greedy for the wealth, power and prestige, which an Israeli-Arab alliance would bring, will seek Israel's destruction for their own personal gain, thus triggering the beginning of the Tribulation!

THE TIMES OF THE GENTILES

When Israel rejected God as their King they also rejected the lasting peace only He could give. The only national peace Israel could enjoy was peace made through alliances with other Gentile nations. It was these alliances that caused the downfall of the kingdom of Israel and of Judah. Likewise, it will be the making of such alliances by the modern State of Israel that will usher in the Tribulation. Thinking they are signing a covenant of peace with the nations, Israel will find out too late they have signed a covenant of death.

The prophet Ezekiel indicated that Israel would be brought into existence because of the actions of the Gentile nations (Ezekiel 38:8). The prophet Daniel indicated that the Tribulation would begin with the confirmation of a covenant between

Israel and the Gentile nations (Daniel 9:27). During the Tribulation the Gentile nations will be judged because of their failure to keep their covenants (contracts) with the nation of Israel.

When God allowed the city of Jerusalem to fall into the hands of the Gentile king, Nebuchadnezzar, He did so with a specific prophetic plan in mind. This event began a period of time called "the times of the Gentiles." This phrase occurs only once in the Bible. It is used by Jesus (see Luke 21:24, NASV). He stated: ". . . Jerusalem will be trampled under foot by the Gentiles until the times of the Gentiles be fulfilled."

Since Jesus used the phrase, "times of the Gentiles," it must have great prophetic significance. A close examination of Scripture reveals that all major prophetic events that transpire here on earth, except for the Messianic Kingdom, take place during the "times of the Gentiles." The times of the Gentiles began in 586 BC with the destruction of the city of Jerusalem. It will conclude when the Messiah, the Lord Jesus, returns to establish His kingdom. The times of the Gentiles is the name Jesus gave to this great span of time when the Gentile nations of the world gain dominion and control over Jerusalem—during which time His offer of blessing and salvation is extended to Jew and Gentile alike.

Today, while Jerusalem has been declared the capital of Israel, and is celebrating its 3000th anniversary, there is uncertainty as to whether or not Jerusalem will remain under Israeli control in the future. Scripture reveals that Israel will certainly lose control of Jerusalem during the Tribulation (see Revelation 11:1–2). It may very well be that one of the peace treaties the modern State of Israel will be forced to sign will guarantee the internationalization of the city of Jerusalem.

There is another reason this span of time is called the "times of the Gentiles." In His prophetic plan, God has used the Gentile nations of the world as His rod of chastisement to the disobedient, rebellious nation that rejected Him as King. To accomplish this, God sent Israel into exile (the Diaspora). But the dispersion was also an act of God's grace, for in the Diaspora God used the Jewish people as a "light unto the nations" (see Romans 9–11).

A NEW COVENANT

God cannot break His Word, it must come to pass. He had promised to establish an everlasting kingdom with the house of David. His promise guaranteed that the dispersion of Israel would be temporary. His covenant guaranteed that Israel would one day return to their land.

God's sovereign plan for Israel has been to use Israel as "a light unto the nations." He accomplished this, in part, by sending Israel into exile. Israel's judgment brought a knowledge of God and salvation to the Gentile nations among whom they were scattered (see Romans 9–11). However, Israel's continued sin among the nations dimmed their light and contributed to the continuous hatred and persecution they have received at the hands of the Gentile nations. Their failure to live for God among the nations would have utterly destroyed them had God not intervened.

Scripture states, "when the fulness of time came, God sent forth His Son" (see Galatians 4:4, NASV). What Israel failed to accomplish, God accomplished through His Messiah, the Lord Jesus. He was a light for all the nations of the world (see Isaiah 9:1–7). Coming through the seed of Abraham, Isaac and Jacob, Jesus literally fulfilled God's promise to Abraham that through his seed all families of the earth would be blessed (see Galatians 3:6–9). Through the Messiah, Jesus, all the nations of the world, including Israel, have found blessing.

During His last Passover feast with His disciples, Jesus revealed that God was making a new contract (covenant) with the house of Israel and Judah—a uni-lateral (unconditional) covenant (see Luke 22:15–20). God fulfilled its terms at Calvary. In His death, burial and resurrection, the Messiah, the Lord Jesus, paid in full mankind's debt for their sins. God accepted the payment, inaugurating Israel's New Covenant with its extended blessing to the Gentile nations of the world (see Jeremiah 31:31–37; Romans 3:21–30; 5:6–21; 2 Corinthians 5:14–21 Hebrews 8:6-13; 12:24).

After His death, burial and resurrection, and before He ascended into heaven, the disciples of Jesus asked Him if He was finally going to restore the kingdom to Israel (see Acts 1:6). Instead of answering their question, Jesus responded by saying:

> . . . It is not for you to know times or epochs which the Father has fixed by His own authority; but you shall receive power when the Holy Spirit has come upon you; and you shall be My witnesses both in Jerusalem, and in all Judea and Samaria, and even to the remotest part of the earth (Acts 1:7–8, NASV).

In His answer, Jesus implied that the kingdom would be established, but that the time of its establishment involved the fulfillment of God's prophetic program. That prophetic program included a spiritual kingdom of which they would be a part as soon as the Holy Spirit was given. Jesus then ascended into heaven and the promise was given that He would return from heaven in the very same way He ascended (see Acts 1:11). The return of Jesus from heaven marks the end of the "times of the Gentiles" and the beginning of the glorious future kingdom for Israel.

After the ascension of Jesus into heaven on Shavuoth (Pentecost), the Holy Spirit (God's Shekhinah Presence) returned to earth. He did not return to the Temple in Jerusalem (from which He departed before its destruction in 586 BC). Instead, He returned to indwell all who, by faith, trust Jesus to be their Lord and Savior.

The Jewish disciples and Jesus' followers who believed Him to be the risen Lord and Savior (see Acts 2) were the first to be indwelt. Then, in fulfillment of God's promise of blessing upon the nations and in accordance with His prophetic program, the

Holy Spirit indwelt Gentiles who trusted Jesus to be the risen Lord and Savior (see Acts 10–13).

With the Holy Spirit indwelling both Jews and Gentiles, God created a unique nation within the nations (see 1 Peter 2:1–10). This unique nation comprises individuals who have not only been born of the flesh, but have been born from above (see John 3). Unlike other nations, this unique nation has no ethnic or gender distinction (see Galatians 3:28). It has no national boundaries. It manifests itself as the spiritual kingdom of God on earth. By faith, its citizens serve and worship the invisible and physically absent King. By faith, its citizens seek to keep their King's commandments, awaiting the day when He will physically return to establish His universal kingdom on the earth. Until the King returns, His Holy Spirit indwells each citizen of this unique kingdom, empowering them to serve Him and to obey His commandments (see John 16:13–15).

The establishment of this spiritual kingdom, the Church, in no way abrogated the promises or prophecies concerning a glorious future kingdom for Israel. Rather, the witness of the Church, the Body of Messiah, gives tangible proof that God still has a future program for Israel. Paul expressed this prophetic truth when he wrote:

> For I do not want you, brethren, to be uninformed of this mystery, lest you be wise in your own estimation, that a partial hardening has happened to Israel until the fulness of the Gentiles has come in; and thus all Israel will be saved; just as it is written,
> "The Deliverer will come from Zion,
> He will remove ungodliness from Jacob."
> "And this is My covenant with them,
> When I take away their sins" (Romans 11:25–27, NASV).

Paul indicates that in spite of the fact that Israel has not been the "light unto the Gentile nations" as God intended, and in spite of the fact that God has chosen others from among all nations, including Israel, to be that light, He will still fulfill His covenants with Israel. The Messiah, the Deliverer, will return and establish the glorious future kingdom promised to Israel.

THE REBUILDING OF JERUSALEM

Nearly 2,000 years have passed since the disciples watched as Jesus ascended into heaven and since they heard the voice of the angel telling them He would return to stand upon the Mount of Olives (see Acts 1:11–12; compare Zechariah 14:4).

The Good News message that salvation is a free gift to all (Jews and Gentiles) because of Jesus' death, burial and resurrection has spread throughout the world. God's unique nation within the nations, the Church, is now composed of believers from among all the nations of the world, including Israel. No one knows how long the Church, (the body of Messiah, the Lord's spiritual kingdom), has to complete its mission of being a "light unto the nations," but a clue is given in the words of Jesus when He said: " . . . and Jerusalem will be trampled underfoot by the Gentiles until the times of the Gentiles be fulfilled" (Luke 21:24, NASV).

Jerusalem was trampled underfoot by the Romans and by other nations until the Israeli army was able to capture and liberate the city in June 1967. After liberating the city, Israel began a vigorous program of rebuilding and beautification, and the nation is now proudly celebrating Jerusalem's 3000th year anniversary.

Scripture is very specific about the final destruction and desecration of Jerusalem. Bible prophecy states that it happens during the last 3-1/2 years of the Tribulation (see Revelation 11:1–2; Daniel 9:26–27). The prophets further state that Jerusalem, as a city, plays an important role in the events of the Tribulation (see Zechariah 12:2–13). In order for these events to take place, Jerusalem must be rebuilt prior to the Tribulation. This is in keeping with the prophet Daniel who foretold of a

ruthless king (the anti-Christ) establishing his palace in Jerusalem (see Daniel 11:45).

It would appear that the capture of Jerusalem in 1967, and
its subsequent rebuilding, is a necessary step in the fulfillment of end-time prophecy. If this is so, it would also appear
that God is setting the stage of world history to fulfill the
times of the Gentiles.

WHAT HAPPENS TO THE CHURCH

Bible scholars disagree over God's future program for the
Church. One major point of dispute is the differing views regarding the rapture of the Church. The four prevalent views are:

1. The Church will be the evangelists of the gospel up to, and
    through, the entire seven year Tribulation; it will then be
    raptured. This view is called the Post-Tribulation view.
2. The Church will be the evangelists for only the first half of
    the Tribulation. This is called the Mid-Tribulation view.
3. The Church will be the evangelists of the gospel for nearly
    three-quarters of the Tribulation, or until God pours out His
    wrath upon Israel and the nations. This view is called the
    Pre-Wrath view.
4. The Church will complete its mission before the Tribula-
    tion begins, and will not experience the Tribulation at all.
    This is called the Pre-Tribulation view. The debate over
    which view is correct has been going on for many years.

No single verse in the Bible clearly states when the rapture
will take place. Hence, each view is dependent upon the interpretation of a particular verse, or of certain passages of Scripture
to validate its teaching.

While the author holds to the Pre-Tribulation view, he believes that the position individual believers hold regarding the
rapture of the Church should never affect their emphasis for
world wide evangelism to Jews and Gentiles alike, nor should it

affect fellowship with believers who hold differing points of view. One's view of the rapture should never become the "litmus" test used to judge whether or not others are true believers.

One's view of the rapture does, however, affect how one interprets end-time events, and one's interpretation of biblical prophecy as it affects God's program for Israel and the Church.

Simply put, the Pre-Tribulation view sees Israel, not the Church, as God's agency for world evangelism in the Tribulation. The Post-Tribulation view sees the Church, not Israel, as God's agency for world evangelism in the Tribulation. The Mid-Tribulation and the Pre-Wrath views see a combination of the Church and Israel as God's means of world evangelism during the Tribulation.

Another obvious distinction between these views is the aspect of judgment. The Pre-Tribulation view believes the Church will be kept from the time of God's wrath. This view holds that the full seven years of the Tribulation are to be viewed as an outpouring of God's wrath, as indicated in the Seal, Trumpet and Vial judgments revealed in the book of Revelation. Sometimes they will make a technical distinction between the first 3-1/2 years and the second 3-1/2 years, or between the Tribulation and the *Great* Tribulation, demonstrating the intensity of God's wrath during the last 3-1/2 years.

Individuals who hold to the Post-Tribulation view believe the Church should undergo persecution, and are not exempt from God's wrath until they are with Him. They believe that all believers need to prepare themselves to go through the entire Tribulation.

Those who hold to the Mid-Tribulation view, or the Pre-Wrath view, attempt to distinguish at what point the wrath of God will be poured out during the Tribulation. They believe the Church will suffer persecution and a part of the judgment of God in the Tribulation, but will be taken out (raptured) before God's wrath is revealed, or before the *Great* Tribulation begins.

There are, of course, many other distinctions and arguments for and against each view, and each view has different ramifications affecting God's prophetic program. The obvious distinctions stated are to demonstrate that no matter which view one holds of the rapture, the Bible clearly states that the rapture of believers must take place in order to fulfill God's prophetic program and in order to change mortality into immortality (see 1 Corinthians 15:51–58; 1 Thessalonians 4:13–18).

It should also be remembered that the timing of the rapture of the Church has no effect upon the outworking of God's prophetic program for Israel. The rapture does not begin the Tribulation. The Tribulation begins with the signing of a covenant. The rapture completes the Church, God's spiritual kingdom on earth. God has set the timing for the beginning of the Tribulation, and He alone has set the time for the return of the Lord Jesus (see Matthew 24:36). Whether the rapture occurs before, during, or at the end of the Tribulation has no bearing upon its events or consequences.

Certainly the rapture of the Church, a mass disappearance of a great part of the human population, will have a profound effect upon the economic, political and religious climate of the world when it happens (unless it takes place according to the post-tribulation view). However, since God's prophetic program for Israel is fixed by His unchangeable decree, the events of the Tribulation and of the kingdom will take place as He has promised in His Word.

Despite differing views on end time events, Christians will agree that God calls on the members of His Church, the Body of Christ, to refrain from the enticements of evil, from the desires of the flesh and a wicked world system to live righteous and holy lives in this world.

THE MESSIANIC WOES

The Lord Jesus told His disciples that the events leading up to the Tribulation would be preceded by "birth-pangs," or by what the rabbis call "the Messianic Woes." According to Jesus, the Messianic woes (or birth-pangs) that will usher in the Tribulation are characterized by false Messiahs, by nations rising against nations and kingdoms against kingdoms, and by famines and earthquakes in various places (see Matthew 24:5–8).

The rabbis of Talmud described the Messianic woes in this way:

> R. Eliezer the Great says: From the day the temple was destroyed, the sages began to be like school-teachers, school-teachers like synagogue-attendants, synagogue-attendants like common people, and the common people [49b] became more and more debased; and there was none to ask, none to inquire. Upon whom is it for us to rely? Upon our Father who is in heaven. In the footsteps of the Messiah, insolence will increase and honour dwindle; the vine will yield its fruit [abundantly] but wine will be dear; the Government will turn to heresy and there will none [to offer them] reproof; the meeting-place [of scholars] will be used for immorality; Galilee will be destroyed, Gablan desolated, and the dwellers on the frontier will go about [begging] from place to place without anyone to take pity on them; the wisdom of the learned will degenerate, fearers of sin will be despised, and the truth will be lacking; youths will put old men to shame, the old will stand up in the presence of the young, a son will revile his father, a daughter will rise against her mother, a daughter-in-law against her mother-in-law, and a man's enemies will be the members of his household; the face of the generation will be like the face of a dog, a son will not feel ashamed before his father. So upon whom is it for us to rely? Upon our Father who is in heaven (Talmud: Sotah 49a–49b).

There are striking similarities between the words of the rabbis and the events of the first half of the Tribulation as recorded by John in the Revelation (see Revelation 6). There are also striking similarities between the words of Jesus and the words of the rabbis of Talmud, and of the rabbis reflected in this present age. Jesus and the rabbis of Talmud could have been describing the twentieth century—and indeed they were!

The Messianic woes (or birth-pangs) spoken of by Jesus precede the actual events of the Tribulation and, like physical birth-pangs, intensify as the birth approaches. As strange as it may seem, the birth-pangs have been going on since the ascension of Jesus, nearly forty years before the destruction of the Temple in 70 AD.

Neither Israel's glorious future nor the Messianic Kingdom began when Jesus ascended, or when the Holy Spirit was given at Pentecost. Jesus warned His disciples that the age preceding His return would be marked by wars, famines, earthquakes, disease, false teachers, and false prophets and that these conditions would grow worse, ultimately ushering in the Tribulation and giving birth to Israel's glorious kingdom.

A cursory glance through history will confirm that mankind is not living in any type of Messianic kingdom. Since the ascension of Jesus, and the destruction of the Temple, there has been constant warfare among the nations. There have been innumerable false Messiahs. Famines and earthquakes continue to plague mankind despite modern technology and modern medicine. Violence, insolence and hatred have not decreased as men have become more educated, more urban, and more scientifically and technologically advanced. These scourges have, in fact, increased!

THE TRIBULATION

As terrible as the birth-pangs (or Messianic woes) will be, the Scripture declares that the Tribulation will be worse. The intensity of violence, hatred, and destruction during the Tribulation will exceed anything that has ever been experienced by mankind (see Matthew 24:21).

Scripture portrays the Tribulation as the day of Satan's wrath against Israel and the saints of God (see Revelation 12:12–17; 13:7). The Tribulation is also portrayed as the time of the outpouring of God's wrath (see Revelation 6:6–17; 11:18; 15:7; 16:1; 16:19). For this reason, it is often referred to as the Day of the Lord (see Ezekiel 13:5; 30:3; Joel 1:15; 2:1, 11, 31; 3:14; Obadiah 15; Zephaniah 1:7, 14).

It must be remembered, however, that while Satan will be active during the Tribulation, and while he will vent his wrath on Israel and on believers, God is sovereign and in control. The Tribulation is the Day of the Lord, and Satan will be judged at its conclusion.

THE COVENANT OF DEATH

In the aftermath of the destruction of Gog and Magog upon the mountains of Israel, the cry for peace will resound throughout the world (see Ezekiel 39). It would appear that Israel's monumental defeat of the armies from the north, and of their Arab allies, will cause the nations of the world to recognize them as a powerful force among the nations. This will prompt a worldwide cry for a treaty of peace.

The desire for peace will be the earnest motivation of Israel when the signatures are applied to the covenant that will usher in the Tribulation (see Daniel 9:26, 27). Israel will believe they are making a covenant of peace between themselves and their Arab neighbors, in cooperation with the other nations of the world. But instead, it will be a covenant of death and destruction. The anti-Christ will use this covenant as a tool to gain control of Jerusalem.

Because they will not recognize God's hand in the destruction of Gog and Magog, the nations of the world will be astonished and perplexed by Israel's massive destruction of Gog and Magog. Fearing that Israel has developed secret and powerful weapons, the nations of the world will cry out for treaties of peace to be signed with Israel, lest the weapons that destroyed

Gog and Magog be used against them. The belief that any nation controlling such an arsenal of weapons would have the power to control the world will be wide-spread. Israel's victory over Gog and Magog has the potential to make that tiny nation the richest and most powerful nation in the world, and seemingly that is what will happen.

Holding a trump card, it would appear that Israel will use their position of strength and power to insist upon their right to rebuild the Temple as a key condition before they sign a covenant of peace. The Bible makes it clear that the leader of the Gentile nations (who will ultimately become the anti-Christ) and the Arab world will confirm Israel's right to rebuild their Temple on the Temple mount in Jerusalem (see Matthew 24:15; Revelation 11:1–2). It may be that one of the very peace treaties being negotiated today between Israel and her Arab neighbors will be a part of the peace treaty confirmed in the Tribulation.

In our day, the idea of Israel rebuilding their Temple is unthinkable! Arab leaders have made it clear that any attempt by Israel to rebuild the Temple on the Temple mount would trigger an immediate war with the Arab world. However, according to Ezekiel's prophecy, the Arab alliance will be severely wounded in the battle of Gog and Magog, as will the northern and southern nations. What appears as an impossibility today, God will make possible in His perfect timing. Many people had thought Israel would never become a nation again, but God keeps His promises!

The peace achieved through the signing of the covenant between Israel and the leader of the Gentile nations corresponds to John's vision of the beginning of the Tribulation as recorded in the Revelation (see Revelation 6:1–17). John envisions peace being established by conquest, as does the prophet Daniel (see Daniel 11:36–45).

According to John's vision, after the second seal is broken, peace is taken from the earth (Revelation 6:3–4). In order for peace to be taken away, it must first be established.

Daniel sees the conquest of peace being accomplished by a willful king who is the leader of the Gentile nations. According to Daniel's vision, this willful king will worship a god of fortresses—a god not known to his fathers (see Daniel 11:37–38). With the help of a "foreign god" (Satan), he moves his armies into the Middle East.

Already weakened by their defeat in the battle of Gog and Magog, the surrounding Arab nations (along with Edom, Moab, Libya, Ethiopia, and Egypt) will be forced to surrender. The earlier peace covenants and treaties with Israel will have made Jerusalem the wealthiest and most powerful city in the world (see Revelation 17–18). Daniel's prophecy indicates that at this point in time the willful king, having brought the entire Middle East under his control, will begin his assault to make Jerusalem his world capital.

MYSTERY BABYLON, THE GREAT

Some Bible scholars believe that the city referred to as the "Mystery City of Babylon the Great" (see Revelation 17:5) is the ancient city of Babylon that they believe will be revived before or during the Tribulation. However, the Bible makes it clear that Satan will make his headquarters in Jerusalem during the Tribulation. "Mystery Babylon" has been a symbolic name applied to Satan's domain since the time of the building of the tower of Babel.

Satan has been the driving force behind all of the mystery religions of the world. Since his deception of Eve in the Garden of Eden, he has vigorously sought to blind the spiritual eyes of mankind to the truth of God's Word. Interestingly, when the two witnesses are killed during the last half of the Tribulation, John is told: "And their dead bodies *will lie* in the street of the great city which mystically is called Sodom and Egypt, where also their Lord was crucified" (Revelation 11:8, NASV). John is told that the "great city" is Jerusalem. Jerusalem was the place where Jesus was crucified. John is then told the woman he saw, "Mystery Babylon," is ". . .the great city, which reigns over the kings of the earth" (Revelation 17:18, NASV).

Ezekiel indicates that her victory over the forces of Gog and Magog will turn the nation of Israel into a tourist attraction of immense proportions. Peace with her Arab neighbors and the rebuilding of the Temple will add to Jerusalem's wealth and prestige. Lingering fears of Israel's "secret weapons" will continue to make her a powerful nation. By the middle of the Tribulation, Jerusalem will be the most important city in the world. It will have reached a "golden era." Many will believe Israel's glorious kingdom has come, but Jerusalem's golden era will not last.

The willful king's armies will infiltrate the land of Israel. Bolstered by the fact that his troops have not been destroyed like the armies of Gog and Magog, and confident that his "god of fortresses" (Satan) is greater than the God of Israel, or of any secret weapon Israel might have, he will move quickly to capture Jerusalem. He will establish his royal pavilion in Jerusalem, making Jerusalem the capital of the world.

Scripture does not indicate at what point during the Tribulation the willful king will capture the city of Jerusalem. It only states that in the middle of the Tribulation (after 3-1/2 biblical years) he breaks his covenant with Israel (see Daniel 9:26). The Bible also states that, at the same time, Satan will be cast out of heaven (see Revelation 12:1–9). Once cast out of heaven, he will vent his wrath on Israel, seeking to destroy the nation. But God will protect the nation by providing a way of escape into the wilderness, and by providing for the nation for a period of 3-1/2 years (see Revelation 12:12–17). The expression used in Revelation is "times, times and half a time" (see Revelation 12:14; Daniel 7:25; 12:7).

The expression "times, times and half a time" is used symbolically in Scripture in reference to "biblical years." A biblical year is a period of time composed of 360 days (12 lunar months composed of 30 days each). Thus, 3-1/2 biblical years would equal

1260 days. John prophesied that this is the exact period of time the city of Jerusalem will be under the final control of the Gentiles before the destruction of the city (see Revelation 11:2–3).

This period of time, then, corresponds with Daniel's prophecy of the final period of seven (the Tribulation). Daniel's prophecy states that in the middle of the seven year Tribulation (or after 42 months or 1260 days), the Gentile world ruler will break the peace covenant he made with Israel (see Daniel 9:26–27).

Both Daniel and Jesus foretold that the abomination of desolation (a great image of the Gentile world ruler) will be set up in the holy place in the Temple after the covenant has been broken (see Daniel 9:26–27; compare Matthew 24:15; Revelation 13:14–15). The image will have the ability to speak and everyone living in the world will be required to worship it. If they do not, they can be killed (see Revelation 13:15).

Paul reveals that the person behind the image is "a man proclaiming himself to be god" (see 2 Thessalonians 2:3–4). Paul and John state that this Gentile world ruler (revealed as the anti-Christ) receives his power and authority from Satan (see 2 Thessalonians 2:9–10; Revelation 13:2–8).

MODERN TECHNOLOGY IN THE HANDS OF A WICKED MAN

In years past, the events of the Tribulation, as described by John, sounded like science fiction. People wondered how it would be possible to make an image talk. They questioned how any one world leader could force everyone to receive a mark in order to buy and sell. They pondered how it would be possible to keep track of millions of people, and determine whether or not they were worshipping the image of the beast?

Since the end of World War II, and the establishment of the State of Israel in 1948, many fantasies of science fiction have become a reality through the explosion of modern technology. Men have walked on the moon. Unmanned space vehicles have explored vast areas of the known universe, and are now being sent beyond the limits of the known universe. Satellites circle our globe in ever increasing numbers as men strive to expand and improve communication, defense, and weather tracking. Manned satellites circle the globe as plans are being formulated for building space-stations in the near future.

In the hands of honorable men, the inventions of modern technology have the potential for making life easier and safer. New technology has improved our lifestyles and our ways of doing business.

However, in the hands of an evil person, such technology has the potential for creating great harm and destruction. We have experienced this on a small scale in our day. Electronic robbery performed by computer hackers and cell phone thieves has reached epidemic proportions. Their infiltration into the records and files of government, banks, investment firms, credit bureaus and the like has created havoc. Thankfully, the government and law enforcement agencies are constantly working to improve security and safety in the use of this modern technology.

However, suppose there were no law enforcement agencies, courts or government agencies to regulate the use of scientific technology. Suppose the control and use of all such technology had fallen into the hands of a powerful evil ruler—a ruler without conscience, who was empowered by Satan, who worshipped the "god of fortresses." This is the picture of Tribulation society during the last 3-1/2 years, after the anti-Christ takes control.

The small computer chip now being designed for placement under the skin to provide doctors with access to genetic information and the medical history of a patient may, in the Tribulation, be used as a mark of identification. Or perhaps the current satellites circling the globe used to provide information to the visually impaired (allowing them through instant communication and tracking devices to navigate mountain trails as well as city sidewalks) will, in the hands of an evil person, be used as a part of his mark of identification. Today's and tomorrow's technology have the potential of producing nightmarish results if placed in the hands of an evil person

Apart from demonic and satanic activity, the Bible does not state how the anti-Christ will accomplish total control of the one world government and its people, but modern technology does demonstrate that such control is plausible and possible.

144,000 Plus 2

The anti-Christ will be unmasked when he breaks his covenant with Israel during the middle of the Tribulation. Once unmasked, he will set up the abomination of desolation (his image) in the Temple, and will take steps to ensure that all people obey and worship him.

Satan will use the anti-Christ's hatred of the Jewish people and his zeal for protecting his empire in a desperate "last ditch" attempt to destroy the Jewish people and to thereby invalidate the word and promises of God (see Revelation 12:12–13). Under the leadership of the anti-Christ, satanic hatred of the Jewish people (anti-Semitism) will reach its zenith. Ironically, Satan's persecution of the Jewish people is the one thing that will hasten his own demise and the downfall of his empire.

Without God's divine intervention, at this point in the Tribulation, the anti-Christ, empowered by Satan, would destroy the nation of Israel. However, God's promise to Abraham, "And I will bless those who bless you, And the one who curses you I will curse" (see Genesis 12:3, NASV), will stand. God will fulfill His promise to Abraham's descendants in three ways during the Tribulation:

First, He will prepare a place in the wilderness where He will protect and provide for the nation (see Revelation 12:14).

Second, He will seal 12,000 Jewish men from each of the tribes of Israel—making a total of 144,000 Jewish evangelists who will be indwelt and protected by the Holy Spirit of God (see Revelation 7:1–10; 14:1–5).

Third, God will appoint two witnesses who have His authority to prophesy, to perform miracles, and to cause plagues and torment to come upon the people living in the empire of the anti-Christ. Just before the end of the Tribulation, these two witnesses will be killed, but they will be resurrected to life and will ascend into heaven (see Revelation 11:3–12)

Some Bible scholars have suggested that God's place of protection for Israel will be Petra. This seems unlikely given modern weaponry and the geographical changes which Scripture states will take place during the Tribulation.

The 144,000 Jewish evangelists will fearlessly herald the message of the gospel to all nations during the last half of the Tribulation. No harm can come to them. They cannot be killed. They will serve as a "light unto the nations," testifying to God's presence in the world—even though society will be totally controlled by Satan. In the midst of evil, God's mercy will provide a way of escape for all who are willing to trust Him. According to John's vision in the Revelation, many from the nations and from Israel will trust God and will be saved during the Tribulation (see Revelation 7:9–17; 14:12–13).

The identities of the two witnesses who will be testifying to the presence of God in the city of Jerusalem (the very capital of the satanic empowered anti-Christ) are not given in Scripture. Bible scholars have suggested they are Elijah and Moses, or Enoch and Moses. Most likely they will be two Jewish individuals living during the Tribulation whom God will appoint and empower to fulfill His will. Their presence, power and miracles will fulfill God's promise of sending Elijah before the great and terrible day of the Lord (see Malachi 4:5–6). Why two witnesses? They represent the two comings of the Messiah, the Lord Jesus. John, the Baptizer, came in the spirit and power of Elijah, and was rejected, even as the leaders of Israel rejected Jesus (see Matthew 17:10–13). Before Jesus returns to set up the Messianic kingdom for Israel, and before the completion of the Day of the Lord, God will send two witnesses to verify and vindicate His dealings with Israel and the nations. God told Israel: "On the evidence of two witnesses or three witnesses, he who is to die shall be put to

death; he shall not be put to death on the evidence of one witness" (see Deuteronomy 17:6, NASV).

Notice what happens in the city of Jerusalem after the ministry, death, resurrection and ascension of the two witnesses.
Scripture states, "And in that hour there was a great earthquake,
and a tenth of the city fell; and seven thousand people were
killed in the earthquake, and the rest were terrified and gave
glory to the God of heaven" (Revelation 11:13, NASV).

The 144,000, plus the two witnesses, validate God's presence in the Tribulation and vindicate that His prophetic program of redemption and judgment for Israel and the nations is
being fulfilled.

THE CAMPAIGN OF ARMAGEDDON

The leader of the Gentile nations, to his great dismay, will
discover too late that the master of deception, Satan, has de-
ceived him. He will realize that his contract with the Devil has
backfired and that he must pay the consequences. As his vast
empire begins to crumble, he will be powerless to stop it.

Scripture reveals that God will pour out His fury and vent
His wrath on the empire of the anti-Christ during the last 3-1/2
years of the Tribulation. God's judgment is symbolized in the
sounding of seven trumpets and in the pouring out from seven
bowls (vials). Only the 144,000 and the two witnesses will be
exempt from the fury of these judgments.

The law and order established during the first half of the
Tribulation will be turned into anarchy during the second half.
Death, destruction, disease, demons, supernatural judgments and
plagues will torment those living on the earth. The abysses of
the deep will be opened, and demonic spirits will be turned loose
(see Revelation 9:1–11). The armies of the world will move toward the Middle East in an effort to put an end to the calami-
tous reign of the Gentile ruler whom they now hold responsible
for the horrendous plagues tormenting mankind. Since the anti-
Christ will be ruling from Jerusalem, the capital of the world

during the Tribulation, the nation of Israel, and the Jewish people will likewise be blamed. History will once again repeat itself. The Jewish people will once again be held accountable for the disasters plaguing the world, just as they were by the Crusaders and Hitler, and atrocities will be again brought upon the Jewish people. Anti-Semitism will reign supreme!

The Bible states that armies from the east, from the north, and from the south will converge on Israel (see Daniel 11:40, 44; Revelation 9:14–16; 16:12), encamping in the great Jezreel Valley in the shadow of the ancient city of Megiddo (see Revelation 16:12–16). From there, they will launch an invasion against the city of Jerusalem, and will completely surround the city (see Joel 3:1–17; Zechariah 12:2; 14:12–14). Along with the others, the descendants of Ishmael and Edom will be there— still hoping to gain possession of the land through the sword rather than through trusting in the promises of God (Amos 1:11; Obadiah 19–21).

The command to invade the city of Jerusalem will go forth to the armies of the earth but it will never be carried out! At the very moment the command is given, the angel of God will pour out the last and final plague upon mankind. John paints the picture in the Revelation. He states:

> And the seventh angel poured out his bowl upon the air; and a loud voice came out of the temple from the throne, saying, "It is done." And there were flashes of lightning and sounds and peals of thunder; and there was a great earthquake, such as there had not been since man came to be upon the earth, so great an earthquake was it , and so mighty. And the great city was split into three parts, and the cities of the nations fell. And Babylon the great was remembered before God, to give her the cup of the wine of His fierce wrath. And every island fled away, and the mountains were not found. And huge hailstones, about one hundred pounds each, came down from heaven upon

men; and men blasphemed God because of the plague of the hail, because its plague was extremely severe (Revelation 16:17–21, NASV).

John's vision compresses the events of Armageddon. This is important to notice, especially in light of the details of Armageddon mentioned elsewhere in Scripture. John says there will be a great earthquake—greater than any earthquake mankind has ever experienced. This earthquake will be so strong that the great city, called Babylon the Great, will be split into three parts, and its citizens will come under God's wrath. Notice the expression used to describe the great city. John writes, "and the cities of the nations [Gentiles] fell" (Revelation 16:19, NASV). This expression identifies the great city Jerusalem as one of the cities of the Gentiles (see Revelation 11:1–3). As indicated earlier, Jerusalem will be under the Gentile leadership of the nations during the Tribulation. Gentile control of Jerusalem will end when the times of Gentiles ends—when the Lord Jesus returns to establish His kingdom (see Luke 21:24).

John also describes a great hailstorm, with hail weighing 100 pounds that maims and kills mankind. He also declares that great topographical changes will take place as islands and mountains disappear as God unshackles His creation from the curse in preparation for the glorious kingdom.

In Scripture the final battle is called "the war of the great day of God, the Almighty" (See Revelation 16:14, NASV), but it is commonly referred to as the Battle of Armageddon. It is a war that will be over before it really begins! According to Scripture, the Lord Jesus will return to earth with the armies of heaven (see Revelation 19:11–21). John wrote: "And I saw the beast [the anti-Christ] and the kings of the earth and their armies, assembled to make war against Him who sat upon the horse, and against His army" (Revelation 19:19, NASV). The armies of the earth that have converged upon Israel to unseat the anti-Christ, will now unite in a desperate attempt to fight against the

Lord Jesus. Their fear of the Lord Jesus will be greater than their fear and hatred of the evil Gentile world ruler! Jesus said of that day:

> But immediately after the tribulation of those days the sun will be darkened, and the moon will not give its light, and the stars will fall from the sky, and the powers of the heavens will be shaken, and then the sign of the Son of Man will appear in the sky, and then all the tribes of the earth will mourn, and they will see the Son of Man coming on the clouds of the sky with power and great glory (Matthew 24:29–30, NASV).

Imagine the terror of seeing the sun and moon blacked out, of seeing stars falling from the heavens, of feeling the earth heave and tremble, opening giant chasms and unleashing molten rivers which crush and kill as they flow.

Against the backdrop of the total darkness, imagine the radiance of the Son of Man (God's Shekhinah Glory) as He returns to earth with the armies of heaven.

One would think that the warriors from around the world who had converged on Israel to capture and destroy the anti-Christ, would drop to their knees and pay homage to the One who returns to earth in such glory. However, this is not the case. Instead, the rulers of the earth, the beast (anti-Christ), his false prophet, and all of their followers will unite along with all of their armies in one last effort to stop the "intruder" from outer space!

However, God cannot be stopped by the armies of mankind! His prophetic program cannot be changed by Satan! In fulfillment of His promise, the Lord Jesus will return to the Mount of Olives (see Zechariah 12:1–9; 14:1–6). Scripture tells us that when His foot touches the Mount of Olives it will split into two pieces from east to west (see Zechariah 14:4). This is the great earthquake which John describes—an earthquake that will divide the city of Jerusalem into three sections (see Revelation 16:19). The armies of the nations and the armies of the anti-Christ will be bunkered in the valleys surrounding Jerusalem. Scripture states that from their positions in the valleys of Jehoshaphat (the Kidron valley), they will be destroyed (see Joel 3:12–16; Zechariah 12:2–6; 14:6). The Lord Jesus will then strike the armies of the Arab world who are gathered in Edom (see Isaiah 63:1–4). Next, He will strike the armies of the nations and of the kings of the earth who are gathered together at Har-Megiddo (see Revelation 16:14–16; 17:14; 19:17–21).

Notice the progression of the campaign of Armageddon. It begins in Jerusalem. From there it spreads to the mountains of Judah, Edom and Moab. From Judah, Edom and Moab it spreads north to the Jezreel Valley, to Meggido. The progression of the battle symbolizes the Lord's cleansing of the land of Israel in preparation for the Kingdom.

The Bible does not state the length of the battle, but it would appear that it is a *blitzkrieg* operation. The words of Jesus give a clue. He said: "For just as the lightning comes from the east, and flashes even to the west, so shall the coming of the Son of Man be" (Matthew 24:27, NASV). Evidently the war is over before it ever really begins!

PAYBACK TIME

The Tribulation is not just a demonstration of God's judgment upon sin and unrighteousness, or a time for the unveiling of God's wrath upon all who refuse to accept His Son as their Lord and Savior. It is a period of time during which He also demonstrates His grace, mercy and long-suffering.

Throughout the seven years of Tribulation, God will continue to extended His grace and mercy to individuals who will trust Him. Through the ministry of the 144,000 and the two witnesses, many from among the nations and from Israel will accept the Lord Jesus. Some who do will be martyred for their faith. Others will suffer great persecution because of their faith.

However, all who are faithful to God's Word, all who refuse to worship the beast (anti-Christ) or to receive his mark, will be rewarded by God.

However, the outcome will be markedly different for those who worship the beast. Individuals who receive his mark and who thus join with the forces of evil to persecute Israel and the believers in the Tribulation, and who fight against God when the Lord Jesus returns, will be killed by the brightness of His coming. John wrote: "And the rest were killed with the sword which came from the mouth of him who sat upon the horse, and all the birds were filled with their flesh" (Revelation 19:21, NASV).

The sword represents the Word of God (see Hebrews 4:12; Revelation 1:16). God's Word and His promises *will not* and *cannot* be broken. Death is the judgment, the payback for sin. All who follow and worship the beast (anti-Christ) knowingly refuse God's payment for sin, the Lord Jesus. They will therefore be slain as a testimony of their sin and unbelief in the God of Abraham, Isaac and Jacob. These individuals, along with all unbelievers who have died throughout the ages of time, will later stand before the Great White Throne of God. At the Great White Throne of God, each will be judged according to their deeds. None will merit life! Not one will have their name written in the Lamb's book of life. Because they have no savior for their sins, each one will be cast into the lake of fire (see Revelation 20:11–15).

John also saw the judgment of the beast (anti-Christ), the false prophet and Satan. During the battle of Armageddon, the beast and the false prophet are seized by the Lord Jesus and thrown alive into the lake of fire (see Revelation 19:20). According to Scripture, the beast (anti-Christ) and the false prophet are the first ones to be placed there. The severity of their sin and rebellion against God were manifest in the Tribulation. By their own actions, they judged themselves and brought condemnation upon themselves. The Lake of Fire is the final judgment of God and there is no escape or reprieve.

According to Scripture, Satan will be cast into the lake of fire after the 1000 year Messianic Kingdom (see Revelation 20:10). The rest of sinful mankind will be cast into the lake of fire following the Great White Throne judgment (see Revelation 20:11–15).

FAITH REWARDED

As has been stated, there will be believers living in the Tribulation—men and women who will trust in God. These individuals will be cared for and protected by God through the ministry of the 144,000 Jewish evangelists. Many Gentiles will come to faith in Jesus as a result of the ministry of the 144,000 (see Revelation 7:4–14).

Living through the days of the Tribulation will be difficult beyond our comprehension and the difficulty will be compounded for believers. Throughout the seven year period, believers (Jews and Gentiles) will be forced to create an underground network just to survive. Because of the horrendous conditions brought about by the judgments of God, as well as by man's inhumanity to man, believers will be called upon to demonstrate their faith through their actions—feeding, clothing, helping those in need—even if helping means jeopardizing their own lives (see Revelation 14:12–13; Matthew 24:13–14; 25:31–46).

Life for believers in the Tribulation will be exceedingly difficult, but not without hope! Believers in the Tribulation will know the Word of God. They will be looking for the Lord Jesus to come (see Matthew 24:32–51)!

While they will not know the day or the hour of His appearance, they will know with unwavering certainty that He will appear! Their certainty will be based upon their faith in the Word of God, and by the very events they are experiencing. When they see the abomination of desolation set up in the Holy Place, they will know they are at least half way through the Tribulation (see Matthew 24:15; Daniel 9:26-27). Being familiar with

Scripture, they will be able to approximate the length of the last half of the Tribulation. It would be impossible for them to know the exact day when the Tribulation commenced, or the exact day of the Abomination of Desolation in the Holy Place of the Temple, for Scripture states that this period of time could be anywhere from 1260 days to 1335 days (see Daniel 12:11–12). It would also be difficult for them to date these events because of the difficulty of measuring time during the Tribulation (see Matthew 24:22; Revelation 6:12–13; 8:12). Thus, believers in the Tribulation, like believers in our own day, will live by faith, trusting God to fulfill His promises and looking for His glorious appearance at any moment of the day or night!

When the Lord Jesus returns in the clouds of heaven, His glory will shine with the brilliance of a million suns. Every eye will see Him (see Revelation 1:7)! As has been stated, the enemies of God will be killed by the brightness of His coming, but for believers His coming will be cause for great rejoicing (see Zechariah 12:10).

However, as God sends His angels to gather His elect, the rejoicing will be replaced by great mourning as both Jewish and Gentile believers will mourn for family and friends who have not accepted Jesus as Messiah and Savior (see Zechariah 12:10–14; Revelation 1:7).

According to Scripture, God will send His angels to gather His elect. Jesus said: "And He will send forth His angels with a great trumpet and they will gather together His elect from the four winds, from one end of the sky to the other" (Matthew 24:31, NASV).

At the same time, the Lord will gather together the nations of the world. Scripture states:

> But when the Son of Man comes in His glory, and all the angels with Him, then He will sit on His glorious throne. And all the nations will be gathered before Him; and He will separate them from one another, as the shepherd sepa-

*rates the sheep from the goats; and He will put the sheep
on His right, and the goats on the left (Matthew 25:31–33,
NASV).*

The elect (the sheep—those who demonstrated their faith
in God and in the Lord Jesus through their actions) will be the
ones on the right. They will become citizens of the great and
glorious Messianic Kingdom that the Lord will establish on the
earth. The unbelievers (the goats) will be on the left. They will be
destined for death and the lake of fire (see Matthew 25:34–46).

Having accomplished the task of separating believers from
non believers, God is now ready to establish the glorious kingdom promised to Israel. The promises of God will be kept, and
those who have faithfully trusted Him through the Tribulation
will know the depth of the meaning of the prophecy song written by the Psalmist:

*Why are the nations in an uproar,
And the peoples devising a vain thing?
The kings of the earth take their stand,
And the rulers take counsel together
Against the LORD and against His Anointed:
"Let us tear their fetters apart,
And cast away their cords from us!"
He who sits in the heavens laughs,
The Lord scoffs at them.
Then He will speak to them in His anger
And terrify them in His fury:
"But as for Me, I have installed My King
Upon Zion, My holy mountain."
"I will surely tell of the decree of the LORD:
He said to Me, 'Thou art My Son,
Today I have begotten Thee.
Ask of Me, and I will surely give the nations as Thine
inheritance,*

And the very ends of the earth as Thy possession.
Thou shalt break them with a rod of iron,
Thou shalt shatter them like earthenware.'"
Now therefore, O kings, show discernment;
Take warning, O judges of the earth.
Worship the LORD with reverence,
And rejoice with trembling.
Do homage to the Son, lest He become angry, and you
perish in the way,
For His wrath may soon be kindled.
How blessed are all who take refuge in Him! (Psalm 2:1–12,
NASV).

Chapter 3
THE PROGRAM FOR A GLORIOUS FUTURE

Israel's glorious future will commence after the Lord has re-turned—after His separation of the sheep and the goats (believ-ers from non-believers). Only the "sheep" (believers who have gone through the Tribulation) will be allowed to enter the glori-ous Messianic kingdom. They will enter the kingdom in their natural bodies, with God's promise that they will receive their glorified bodies at the conclusion of the 1,000 year kingdom. Believers who died, or were martyred in the Tribulation be-cause of their faith, will rule and reign with the Messiah in resurrected and glorified bodies during the kingdom (see Revelation 20:4–6).

Believers who lived and died during the Old Testament pe-riod will be resurrected, and will also have a part in the Messi-anic kingdom (see Daniel 12:13). Believers from the Church Age (the period of time beginning at Pentecost and ending with the rapture of the Church) who either died believing in Jesus, or were raptured, will have a part in this glorious kingdom (1 Thessalonians 4:13–18; 1 Corinthians 15:50–54; Revelation 2:26–28; 3:12).

Moreover, how will believers, who enter the kingdom in glorified bodies, interface with believers who have gone through the Tribulation, who enter the kingdom in non-glorified bodies? The answer to this question is not addressed in Scripture. A study of the references to the new city of Jerusalem may shed some light on this matter, and mention of the new Jerusalem will be made later in this chapter.

The length of the earthly Messianic Kingdom has been predetermined by God. It is to last for 1000 years (see Revelation 20:1–10). No reason is given in Scripture as to why the kingdom will last for 1000 years. Perhaps the life spans of Methuselah and Adam provide a clue. Scripture states that Methuselah lived to be 969 years old; Adam lived 930 years (see Genesis 5:5, 27). Consideration must be given to the fact that Adam was created as an adult male. We do not know how old he was at the time of his creation, but one assumption is that he may have been a man of about thirty plus years of age. The Lord Jesus, the last Adam (see Romans 5:12–19; 1 Corinthians 15:45), was thirty years of age when He began His ministry. It is possible, therefore, that the 1000 year kingdom represents the life span of mankind from Adam to Methuselah, plus a biblical generation (between 30 to 40 years).

Why would God choose the period of time from Adam to Methuselah? Adam was created by God and lived in the Garden of Eden—Paradise. He experienced life before God placed a curse upon the earth. Methuselah, on the other hand, experienced life after the curse. He never experienced Paradise on earth. According to biblical chronology, he died in the same year God judged the world by sending the great flood.

During the Kingdom, the curse will be lifted from the earth and paradise will be restored. Yet despite the perfect conditions and the presence of God in the Messianic Kingdom, there will be individuals born during the kingdom who will harden their hearts against God and His truth (see Isaiah 65:20).

Individuals born in the Kingdom who harden their hearts against God and who chose to serve evil, demonstrate the wickedness of the human heart and the depravity of the human spirit. Living at a time when everything is provided by a merciful and loving God, their sinful behavior shows that mankind is worthy of God's judgment. They further demonstrate that mankind is incapable of saving themselves from their own sin nature. Even in the Kingdom, salvation is through faith, based on the grace of God. All who will accept God's grace, and who will willingly submit themselves to the Messiah, the Lord Jesus, will be saved.

During the Messianic Kingdom, mankind will have a knowledge of both good and evil. Just as God created Adam and Eve with free will, individuals will continue to be born with free will. However, the events of the 1000 year Kingdom will be just the reverse of events in the Garden of Eden.

From the inception of the Garden, Satan was permitted to come and go at will; he was permitted to tempt man; man rebelled against God and Paradise was lost. The appearance of Satan in the Garden of Eden brought temptation, sin and death to mankind.

During the Kingdom, Satan will be bound for 1000 years (see Revelation 20:2, 3) and mankind will once again enjoy the conditions of "Paradise." However, even with Satan bound, sin will be present because mankind's sin nature will still be a part of his makeup. Mankind will still have a knowledge of good and evil. Moreover, sin will not bring immediate expulsion from "Paradise" as it did from the Garden. Instead, those who sin will be given opportunity to seek forgiveness from sin, through faith in the Lord Jesus, and healing through the waters of life flowing through the land (see Ezekiel 47:12).

When Satan is released from his prison, he will re-enter Paradise and will once again be permitted to tempt men. In doing so, a great number of those born during the Kingdom will choose to follow him (see Revelation 20:7–10). This time Paradise is *not* lost! Satan and those who follow him will lose and will be immediately judged. The appearance of Satan at the end of the 1000 year Kingdom reign of the Messiah will bring an end to temptation, sin and death to mankind.

While it is true that Satan will lead a rebellion against God after the 1000 year reign of the Messiah, his following will not be a total representation of mankind as it was with Adam and Eve. Adam and Eve had no knowledge of good or evil until, tempted by Satan, they ate of the forbidden fruit (see Genesis 2:9, 16–17; 3:1–13). Scripture does not state explicitly that the majority of people born during the Kingdom will choose righteousness, but it is implied

In many ways the Messianic kingdom is a demonstration of the maturation process for the human race. From the time of Adam, to the establishment of the Messianic Kingdom, Satan's attempts to align mankind with his agenda and with his rebellion against God have been constant. However, during the Kingdom Age mankind will, for the first time, be free from the temptation and deception of Satan. Mankind will be free to curb and control its sin nature by exercising faith and obedience to their King and Messiah, the Lord Jesus. Satan was a defeated foe at Calvary, but the outcome of his attempt to overthrow the Lord Jesus at the end of the 1000 year Kingdom will prove that he will never again regain his control over mankind. Sin will have run its course, and will be forever judged!

THY KINGDOM COME

When the disciples asked the Lord Jesus to teach them to pray, He gave them a model. He said,

> *Pray, then, in this way:*
> *"Our Father who art in heaven,*
> *Hallowed be Thy name.*
> *Thy kingdom come.*
> *Thy will be done,*
> *On earth as it is in heaven.*
> *Give us this day our daily bread.*
> *And forgive us our debts, as we also have forgiven our debtors.*

*And do not lead us into temptation, but deliver us from evil.
[For Thine is the kingdom, and the power, and the glory,
forever. Amen]" (Matthew 6:9–13, NASV).*

This model prayer has application for all ages, but it is a
particularly appropriate prayer in the Messianic kingdom. In the
Kingdom, God's will shall be done on earth—as it is done in
heaven. The Messiah, the Lord Jesus, will rule the nations with
a rod of iron. He will be the merciful and benevolent King who
will act in righteousness toward all of His subjects. Every need of
His subjects will be met. Their daily bread will be supplied just
as He supplied manna to the sons of Israel in the wilderness.

Since the knowledge of God will pervade the whole earth
(see Jeremiah 31:34), the forgiveness of sin will be a reciprocal
act. Jesus said the attitude toward sin and the sinner will be, ". . .
forgive us our debts (moral sins or trespasses), as we also have
forgiven our debtors (those have sinned against us)" (see Matthew 6:12, NASV). The act of granting forgiveness to another
person before asking for God's forgiveness will be the way of life
in the Kingdom (see Matthew 6:15).

The last phrase of this model prayer says, "And do not lead
us into temptation, but deliver us from evil" (Matthew 6:13,
NASV). In the Kingdom, all temptation (except personal temptation brought about by the sin nature that will still be inherent
in mankind during the kingdom) will be removed. Satan will be
bound. Mankind will be delivered from the evil one, as well as
from evil brought about by natural disasters, disease and other
atrocities present in this age and in past ages.

However, before the Kingdom of God (the glorious Messianic kingdom of 1,000 years) is established, the earth must undergo a radical rebirth.

CREATION REBORN

The apostle Paul was anxiously awaiting the day of God's
kingdom on earth when he wrote these prophetic words:

For I consider that the sufferings of this present time are not worthy to be compared with the glory that is to be revealed to us. For the anxious longing of the creation waits eagerly for the revealing of the sons of God. For the creation was subjected to futility, not of its own will, but because of Him who subjected it, in hope that the creation itself also will be set free from its slavery to corruption into the freedom of the glory of the children of God. For we know that the whole creation groans and suffers the pains of child-birth together until now. And not only this, but also we ourselves, having the first-fruits of the Spirit, even we ourselves groan within ourselves, waiting eagerly for our adoption as sons, the redemption of our body (Romans 8:18-23, NASV).

Apparently God's judgment in the Tribulation accomplishes more than simply punishing mankind for their sin. His judgments also have the effect of removing the curse placed on the earth when man sinned—thus bringing about a "rebirth" of creation. In pouring out His wrath, God's justice will be served. In removing the curse, the shackles and restraints placed upon creation by the curse will also be removed, triggering natural disasters. This is why the removal of the curse in the Tribulation is called "birth-pangs."

Paul stated that during this present age all of creation is suffering through the pains of childbirth—until the day it will be reborn. The Tribulation will be the last of the birth-pangs, and the most severe! As seen in the previous chapter, the intensity of God's judgment upon the earth and its inhabitants will cause mountains to fall, oceans and rivers to change or dry up, and stars to fall from heaven.

The prophet Isaiah used these descriptive words: "Behold, the LORD lays the earth waste, devastates it, distorts its surface, and scatters its inhabitants. . . . The earth is broken asunder, The earth is split through, The earth is shaken violently. The earth reels to and fro like a drunkard, And it totters like a shack" (See Isaiah 24:1; 19–20, NASV).

Isaiah describes earth going through its rebirth in preparation for the Kingdom. Out of the chaos of judgment, God will restore the beauty and glory of His creation—a world no longer under His curse and wrath. God will restore the world to the conditions that existed in Eden, where He planted a garden in which to fellowship with the man and woman (see Genesis 2:8–25; 3:8–13).

TOPOGRAPHICAL AND GEOGRAPHICAL CHANGES

The cataclysmic upheaval of the earth during the Tribulation will result in massive changes to the earth's surface—to its seas, lakes, rivers and continents. Although it cannot be stated conclusively, it would appear that there will be a total re-alignment of the continents, perhaps even shifting the continents back into one great land mass surrounded by seas.

The creation account is the picture given of Eden before the fall of man—before God's judgment in the days of Noah and before His judgment at the Tower of Babel (see Genesis 1:9–10; 6:11–24; 11:1–9). God will restore the earth to a state of holiness and beauty that existed before the fall of man.

It would appear that throughout the Kingdom Age, the earth will be covered, or shaded, by a surrounding canopy that will protect the earth and its inhabitants from the ultraviolet rays and intense heat of the sun. In the Kingdom Age, mankind will live in a protected environment (see Zechariah 14:6–7). The prophet Isaiah wrote of Jerusalem in that day, saying:

When the Lord has washed away the filth of the daughters of Zion, and purged the bloodshed of Jerusalem from her midst, by the spirit of judgment and the spirit of burning, then the LORD will create over the whole area of Mount Zion and over her assemblies a cloud by day, even smoke, and the brightness of a flaming fire by night; for over all

the glory will be a canopy. And there will be a shelter to
give shade from the heat by day, and refuge and protec-
tion from the storm and the rain (Isaiah 4:4–6, NASV;
see also Isaiah 60:19–20).

With the curse removed from earth, the Kingdom Age will
be a time when all creation will once again enjoy the Edenic
conditions which existed prior to the fall of man. The earth will
produce abundantly, providing food for everyone (see Amos 9:13-
15; Isaiah 65:21–22). Animals will lose their ferocity and will
co-exist in peace with one another and with mankind (see Isaiah
11:6–9; 35:9; 65:25). The aging process will be slowed down
and mankind will live longer (see Isaiah 65:20). Sickness and
disease will disappear (Isaiah 33:24; Jeremiah 30:17).

When the Lord returns to the Mount of Olives, the mountain will be cut in half from east to west, creating two great mountains—one to the north and one to the south. A great plain and
valley will also be created by this cataclysmic event (see
Zechariah 14:4; 10). Zechariah reveals that the remains of the
city of Jerusalem (remains from the time of David) will be preserved. It is interesting to note that the modern state of Israel
has preserved the ruins of the ancient city of David in our day!
The prophet also indicates that in the topographical and geographical changes that take place, the present city of Jerusalem
will be elevated to the height of the northern plateau that will
be created when the Mount of Olives is divided (see Zechariah
14:10).

The prophets reveal that in the Kingdom, peoples from all
nations will be required to go up to the Temple in Jerusalem to
worship the Lord God (see Isaiah 2:2–4; 60:4–14; Micah 4:1–2).
Clearly, the topographic changes spoken of by the prophets will
be needed to accommodate the rebuilding of the new city of
Jerusalem with its enlarged, magnificent Temple, and to accommodate the increased population (Jew and Gentile) who will
occupy Jerusalem in the Messianic Kingdom.

The high flat-top mountain to the north of the great valley that will be created, will be the site on which the Kingdom Temple will be built. On the southern end of that great mountain, elevated so that it appears to be of equal height, the new city of Jerusalem will be built (see Ezekiel 40:2). Evidently, in the upheaval of the mountains and valleys brought about by the events of the Tribulation and by the return of the Lord Jesus, the present Mount Moriah and Mount Zion will be merged into the part of the Mount of Olives that will shift northward. During the Kingdom, that great mountain is called Mount Zion, or the Holy Mountain of the Lord.

NEW JERUSALEM IN THE KINGDOM

The new city of Jerusalem will be built in the shape of a square. Each side will be 4,500 *rods* long (see Ezekiel 48:30–35). Unfortunately, Ezekiel's description of the new city of Jerusalem has not been easily understood due to the translation of chapter 48. The implication from the Hebrew text is that the measurements should be given in *rods* and not in *cubits* (as the italics of some translations suggest). In Ezekiel 40:5, a *rod* is described as being equal to 6 *cubits*. If one uses the Egyptian *cubit* (which was in use during Ezekiel's time), a *cubit* would equal 20.5 inches. Therefore the measuring *rod* Ezekiel used was approximately 10.25 feet in length (6 x 20.5 inches=123 inches; 123 inches divided by 12 inches=10.25 feet).

Using the *rod* as the means of measurement, each wall surrounding the city will be approximately 8.7 miles in length (4500 *rods* x 10.25 feet=46,125 feet; 46,125 feet divided by 5,280 feet=8.7 miles). The perimeter of the entire city would therefore be approximately 34.9 miles (see Ezekiel 48:35). Each wall— north, south, east and west—will have gates named after the tribes of Israel. The gates of the north wall will be named after Reuben, Judah and Levi. The gates of the east side will be named after Joseph, Benjamin and Dan. The gates of the south side wall will be named after Simeon, Issachar and Zebulun. The

gates of the west side wall will be named after Gad, Asher and
Naphtali (see Ezekiel 48:30–34).

The city of new Jerusalem in the Kingdom will occupy an
allotment of ground south of the Temple. It will comprise a total
area of 5,000 *rods* (approximately 9.7 miles) by 25,000 *cubits*
(approximately 48.53 miles), or 470.7 sq. miles (see Ezekiel 45:6;
48:15–20). This great city will be the capital of the world. It will
be the city where the Prince from the lineage of David will dwell
(see Ezekiel 44:3; 45:16–17; 46:12; 16–18). For this reason, the
city will no longer be called Jerusalem. It will be called "The
LORD is there" (see Ezekiel 48:35, NASV).

To the north of the new city will be a great plateau covering
the entire top of the great mountain. The Kingdom Temple will
stand in the middle of this great plateau—like a beautiful jewel
in a tiffany setting. The prophet Ezekiel states:

> *The allotment that you shall set apart to the LORD shall
> be 25,000 cubits in length, and 10,000 in width. And
> the holy allotment shall be for these, namely for the priests,
> toward the north 25,000 cubits in length, toward the west
> 10,000 in width, toward the east 10,000 in width, and
> toward the south 25,000 in length; and the sanctuary of the
> LORD shall be in its midst (Ezekiel 48:9–10, NASV).*

Once again, using Ezekiel's *rod* as the means of measurement
(replacing the italicized "*cubit*" which is an insertion by translators), the length of the plateau will be approximately 48.53 miles.
The breadth of the plateau will be approximately 19.4 miles.
The perimeter would thus cover an area of approximately 941.5
square miles.

The reason this great plateau is so large is because the Temple
(the sanctuary) will be built in the middle (see Ezekiel 45:4),
with the surrounding area occupied by the sons of Zadok, who
will serve as the priests during the Kingdom Age (see Ezekiel
40:46; 43:19; 44:15; 48:11). Zadok was a high priest during the

reign of David—the eleventh high priest in the descent from Aaron. God promised that his seed would have a prominent place of ministry in the Kingdom (see 1 Kings 1:26, 32–45).

Interestingly, the Scriptures affirm that the Levitical priesthood will also be established in the Kingdom, but they will have limited power because of their apostasy and rebellion against God when the first Temple stood (see Ezekiel 40:46; 43:19; 44:15–31). Because of Zadok's faithfulness to God, the sons of Zadok were appointed to fulfill the Levites' priestly duties. Once again, Scripture reveals that God keeps His promises—to the smallest detail!

In addition to the great area set aside for the sanctuary and for the priests, an additional area measuring 500 *rods* by 500 *rods* (nearly a mile square) is to be set aside as a holy place (see Ezekiel 45:2). Perhaps this area will be used as pasture land for the sacrificial animals.

Throughout the Kingdom Age, this great temple plateau will be the place of worship for Israel and for all of the nations of the world. Each year, during the Feast of Tabernacles (Succoth), all families on the earth will be required to go up to Jerusalem to worship the King, the Lord of Hosts. Failure to do so will result in no rain, symbolically emphasizing a famine, or lack of both physical and spiritual nourishment (see Zechariah 14:16–19).

As has already been mentioned, every need of earth's inhabitants will be supplied by the Lord, the King, in the Kingdom. The King will, however, expect obedience from His subjects and, because mankind's sin nature will not yet be removed and because sin will be present in the Kingdom, He will rule the nations with a rod of iron (see Psalms 2:7–9).

THE TEMPLE IN THE KINGDOM

The Kingdom Temple that will stand in the midst of the great plateau on the holy mountain, will be unique from all previous Temple structures.

1. The Presence of God will be there—confirmed on the basis of the new covenant, established through the death, burial and resurrection of the Messiah, the Lord Jesus. The prophet Ezekiel states:

    And I shall make a covenant of peace with them; it will be an everlasting covenant with them. And I will place them and multiply them, and will set My sanctuary in their midst forever. My dwelling place also will be with them; and I will be their God, and they will be My people. And the nations will know that I am the LORD who sanctifies Israel, when My sanctuary is in their midst forever (Ezekiel 37:26–28, NASV).

2. The Kingdom Temple will be substantially different from all previous temples. Foremost among the differences is the fact that its architectural design will not be like that of previous temples. Its size and decoration will be different. Its gates and courts will be arranged differently. The ways in which the sacrifices and offerings will be made, as well as the celebration of the holy days, will be unlike those of the past. Ezekiel's description of the Kingdom Temple, especially the difference in the architectural design, has perplexed the rabbis of Talmud. Scripture states that the original pattern for the Temple, built by Solomon, was given to David by God and was written down (see 1 Chronicles 28:19).

    The rabbis of Talmud are adamant that these written instructions cannot be changed or modified (see Talmud, Succah 51b). Yet, when one compares the Temple which Solomon built with the ones which Zerubbabel and Herod built, there are significant differences. The rabbis disregard this, suggesting that the phrase "According to all that I am going to show you . . ." (Exodus 25:9, NASV) makes an allowance for future revelations about the form and shape of God's dwelling place on earth. The rabbis make this allowance because of Israel's sin and God's promise to leave His sanctuary if they did not repent.

The Temple Ezekiel describes is distinct from all others in that God declares He will never leave it. It will be the place of His dwelling forever. The architecture, design and worship therefore all reflect the Glory and Presence of God in His dwelling place forever.

3.   The Temple in the Kingdom is also the place of God's Throne (Ezekiel 43:7). No throne was established in the previous temples. When Israel rejected God as their King, God separated the duties of the king and the priests. The throne was to be kept separate from the temple. However, in the Kingdom Temple the King will serve as both king and priest (see Zechariah 6:9–14; Ezekiel 45:17).

4.   The priesthood and worship of the Temple will be presided over by a person called the Prince (see Ezekiel 40:45–46; 42:13–14; 43:19, 24, 27; 44:15, 31; 45:4; 46:2, 19–20; 48:10–11, 13). This Prince is never identified by Ezekiel, and his identity remains a mystery. Perhaps a clue to his identity is given, however, in his duties and responsibilities. Ezekiel states that he will serve as a mediator between the people and the priests. He will perform a servant role, as well as a kingly role—thus fulfilling the promise made to David that his kingdom would last forever (see 2 Samuel 7:12–16).

It is true that this promise finds its ultimate fulfillment in the Messiah, the Lord Jesus. However, there appears to be a partial fulfillment of this promise in the Kingdom in the person designated as the Prince. Ezekiel makes it clear that the Prince cannot be the Messiah, as the Prince is married and has sons (see Ezekiel 46:16). Also, he must make sin

offerings for himself (see Ezekiel 45:22). It would appear that
the Prince fulfills the promise made to David's seed of a house
and throne in Jerusalem, and finds its literal fulfillment in
the Kingdom Age.

5.   Some of the furnishings of previous temples are not men-
     tioned by Ezekiel as being present in the Kingdom Temple.
     There is no mention of the veil that separated the Holy of
     Holies from the Holy Place. There is also no mention of the
     Ark of the Covenant, the Table of Showbread, the Sea of
     Glass, the Menorahs (the lampstands) or the Laver.
     One would think that Ezekiel would have described all of
     these important furnishings in detail. Instead, he details the
     architecture, the design and the gates of the Temple. He
     mentions only an altar of wood that serves as a table before
     the Lord (see Ezekiel 41:22), and the altar hearth with its
     ledge (see Ezekiel 43:15–17; 45:19; 47:1). No other furnish-
     ings are mentioned!

     Perhaps these items were not mentioned because they will
     not be necessary for Temple worship in the Kingdom. Scrip-
     ture says the veil was torn in half when the Lord Jesus was
     crucified (see Matthew 27:51). There is therefore no longer
     a need for the veil in the Temple, as the Lord Jesus is now
     the entrance to the Holy of Holies (see Hebrews 10:19–20).
     This is made clear in the description given to Ezekiel of God's
     presence and glory dwelling within the great Sanctuary.
     Ezekiel wrote that God would set His threshold by their
     threshold and His doorpost next to their doorpost, with only
     the wall of the Temple between God and the sons of Israel
     (see Ezekiel 43:7–9). God says He will dwell with His people
     openly, not hidden in the dark, not separated by a veil. In
     that day, even the bells of horses, the cooking pots, and the
     people themselves will be declared "Holy To The Lord!" (see
     Zechariah 14:20–21, NASV).

Through His death and resurrection, the Lord Jesus symbolically fulfilled the meaning and purpose of all of the Temple and Tabernacle furnishings, worship and sacrificial system, as given by God.

6.   Worship in the Kingdom Temple will be different from worship in the previous Temples. The sacrifices will be a memorial to the death, burial and resurrection of the Messiah, the Lord Jesus, who is the Lamb of God who took away the sin of the world (see John 1:29).

While Ezekiel mentions the keeping of feasts and fasts, the observance of the Sabbath and appointed feasts, and the need for sacrifice to make atonement (see Ezekiel 45:17–20), the prophet mentions only one major feast that all of Israel must keep—Passover, the Feast of Unleavened Bread (see Ezekiel 45:21–25).

Interestingly, Passover is also the only feast memorialized in the Church. At His last Passover, Jesus took the bread and wine and used them to symbolize his death, burial and resurrection (see Luke 22:7–20). That part of the Passover service has been kept by the Church as its memorial feast (communion) (see 1 Corinthians 11:23–29). In the kingdom, Passover will be kept as a continuing memorial to the price God paid to redeem mankind unto Himself.

One would think that Ezekiel would have mentioned Israel's most important feast day—Yom Kippur (the Day of Atonement), but he does not. Perhaps the reason is that Yom Kippur was the time when God renewed His annual contract with Israel to dwell in their midst. Each year the high priest would make the Yom Kippur sacrifice for the nation, and would enter into the holy of holies (see Leviticus 16:1–34). In His death, burial and resurrection, the Messiah, the Lord

Jesus, made atonement for the sin of all mankind (see Hebrews 9:1–10:22). In the Kingdom, Israel will be living under the terms of the New Covenant (see Jeremiah 31:31–34). God promised that He would dwell among them forever (see Ezekiel 43:7). Therefore, in the Kingdom, the terms of the Old Covenant will no longer apply; the meaning and obligation of sacrifice, worship, and keeping of the holy days, fasts and feasts, as they applied under the Old Covenant, will no longer be necessary.

7. Unlike all previous temples, healing waters will flow from under the Kingdom Temple, flowing eastward to the Dead Sea (see Ezekiel 47:1-12). This is by far one of the most distinguishing features of the Kingdom Temple. This great Temple will stand high above the surrounding plains and valleys. From its base, flowing under the altar of sacrifice and out from the East gate, will come living waters! As this water cascades down the mountainside, it will become a great river in the lower valley. The river will flow eastward, giving life to everything it touches. Finally, the great river will flow into the salty marshes of the Dead Sea; however, instead of changing the marshes into groves of living trees and plants, the water allows the marshes to remain and to continue supplying salt. The river then dumps into the Dead Sea, and the sea comes alive with fish and living creatures. The prophet is then told:

"And by the river on its bank, on one side and on the other, will grow all kinds of trees for food. Their leaves will not wither, and their fruit will not fail. They will bear every month because their water flows from the sanctuary, and their fruit will be for food and their leaves for healing" (Ezekiel 47:12, NASV).

This great river will supply food, medicines, "salt" and the necessities of life for everyone living in Israel. The river will be the means God uses to fulfill His promise of a glorious Kingdom for Israel.

The prophet Zechariah also spoke about this river, adding a few more details. He says, "In that day a fountain will be opened for the house of David and for the inhabitants of Jerusalem, for sin and for impurity" (Zechariah 13:1, NASV). This great flowing river will be a sign throughout the Kingdom Age that God has purified Israel and that Israel, as a nation, will now worship and serve Him.

Zechariah also says: "And it will come about in that day that living waters will flow out of Jerusalem, half of them toward the eastern sea and other half toward the western sea; it will be in summer as well as in winter" (Zechariah 14:8, NASV). Notice that Zechariah says the great river will not only flow east, toward the Dead Sea, but that it will also flow west, toward the Mediterranean sea. Thus, the whole of the land of Israel will be watered by the living waters that will flow through a valley created when the Messiah, the Lord Jesus returns—when the touch of His foot splits the Mount of Olives in two (see Zechariah 14:4).

At the end of the Tribulation this valley will provide Israel with safety and protection from her enemies. Israel will be saved by passing through the valley which God will create when the Lord Jesus returns. In the Kingdom, Israel will be kept by the living waters that will flow through the great valley. God will faithfully keep His promises so that all Israel can be saved (see Romans 11:25–27).

8. The Eastern Gate (the Golden Gate, or Mercy Gate) leading to the sanctuary will be sealed during the Kingdom Age (see Ezekiel 44:1–3). The Eastern Gate is the gate leading

to the Mount of Olives. When the Messiah, the Lord Jesus, returns to the Mount of Olives, it will be split in half and one part will comprise the great plateau on which the Temple will be built. Ezekiel is told that the Eastern Gate will remain shut because the Lord of Glory passed through it (see Ezekiel 44:2).

The sealing of the Eastern Gate will be a visual reminder to the citizens of the Messianic Kingdom of the promises of God. God promised a glorious kingdom to Israel and He promised that the Lord Jesus would return to the Mount of Olives and establish that glorious kingdom (see Acts 1:11–12; Ezekiel 43:1–5).

When the first and second Temples stood in Jerusalem, the Eastern Gate remained opened. However, after the destruction of the Temple and Moslem control of the Temple site, the Eastern Gate was sealed! Believing that the Jewish Messiah would not defile Himself, and thus ensuring that the gate would remain closed, Moslem religious authorities have placed a graveyard outside the Eastern Gate. All of this was done in an attempt to maintain Moslem control over the Temple Mount.

Neither man nor Satan can invalidate the Word of God. Jesus will return as promised. The Temple will stand on the great mountain throughout the Kingdom Age and the Eastern Gate will remain shut as a testimony to the fact that God keeps His covenants!

THE DIVISION OF THE LAND

In the Kingdom, all Israel will be re-gathered to the land promised to Abraham, Isaac and Jacob (see Isaiah 27:12–13). The Diaspora will be over! There will be no Jewish people in exile; none will be found living among the Gentile nations (see

Deuteronomy 30:1–5). However, Gentiles, too, will be welcome to live in the land of Israel, as will the descendants of Ishmael. Ezekiel wrote these amazing words:

> "And it will come about that you shall divide it [the land] by lot for an inheritance among yourselves and among the aliens who stay in your midst, who bring forth sons in your midst. And they shall be to you as the native-born among the sons of Israel; they shall be allotted an inheritance with you among the tribes of Israel. And it will come about that in the tribe with which the alien stays, there you shall give him his inheritance," declares the Lord GOD (Ezekiel 47:22–23, NASV).

According to Isaiah, because the land given to Israel extends into Egypt, the Egyptians will come to know the Lord (see Isaiah 19:21). Likewise, the Assyrians will come to know the Lord (see Isaiah 19:23–25). The land given to Israel in the Kingdom will be large enough to support Jews, Arabs, Egyptians and other Gentiles from among the nations.

To accommodate worship and communication, God will restore a pure language to the people. There will no longer be the confusion of tongues caused by God's judgment at the time of the building of the Tower of Babel. All inhabitants of the Kingdom will speak the same language (see Zephaniah 3:9).

The prophet Ezekiel states that in order to properly govern and administrate the great numbers of people living in the land, the land will be divided, or allotted, by tribe. The allotments assigned to each of the tribes of Israel will result in a full occupation of the land promised under the terms of God's contract with Abraham, Isaac and Jacob.

Seven of the tribes of Israel will occupy land to the north of the great Temple square, and five of the tribes will occupy the land south of the great Temple square. The Levites and the sons of Zadok will occupy land immediately surrounding the great

Temple square, along with an allotment given to the Prince.

The allotments will be large squares of land. In the north, the allotments begin with the tribe of Dan, followed by Asher, Naphtali, Manasseh, Ephraim, Reuben and Judah, who has a common border with the great Temple square. In the south, the allotments begin with Benjamin, who has a common border with the great Temple square, and continue with Simeon, Issachar, Zebulun, and Gad (see Ezekiel 48:1–29).

The allotment given to each tribe, with the exceptions of Judah, Benjamin and Gad, is identical to their original placement in the land. No explanation is given as to why Judah, Benjamin, and Gad are not given their original placement in the Kingdom allotment. Any attempt to explain this change would be purely conjecture. It is likely, however, that the changes in placement have to do with the great Temple square (*Terumah*). The allotments given to Benjamin and Judah border the *Terumah* on the north and on the south. The land dedicated to the Prince borders the *Terumah* on the east and west. The kings of Israel came from the tribes of Benjamin and Judah. Their placement around the sacred *Terumah*, along with that of the Prince, is a reminder of God's fulfilled promises.

Each tribe will receive a strip of land 25,000 *rods* long, with its width determined by the Mediterranean Sea to the west and the Euphrates river to the east. Given these measurements, and converting the *rods* to miles, the size of the land occupied by the seven tribes in the north is approximately 339.7 miles north to south, with the northern border extending to Mount Hermon (see Ezekiel 48:1). The five tribes to the south would occupy a strip of land approximately 243 miles long, extending south to the river of Egypt (see Ezekiel 48:28).

It must be remembered that the great Temple plateau and the city of Jerusalem occupy another strip of land 25,000 *rods* by 25, 000 *rods* (48.5 miles by 48.5 miles). This means there will be 13 allotments (strips of land) 48.5 miles in length, extending from the Mediterranean Sea to the Euphrates River west to east.

Putting these strips of land together gives the boundaries of the promised land in the Kingdom. The length of the land to the north will be: 7 tribes @ 48.5 miles each=339.5 miles. The sacred Temple square (the *Terumah*): 1 x 48.5 miles=48.5 miles. The length to the south: 5 tribes @ 48.5 miles=242.5 miles. The total land from north to south would therefore equal 630.5 miles.

Placing these measurements on a map of the Middle East shows that the land allocated to the tribes of Israel more than equals the land from Mount Hermon to the Euphrates River to the Nile River in Egypt. God will change the topography and geography of the world to accommodate His Messianic Kingdom.

Evidently, in the Kingdom, some rivers, mountains and seas will be identified by their historic names, and will serve as landmarks—reminders of the past and of the faithfulness of God in keeping His promises.

Interestingly, the Tigress and Euphrates rivers are said to be among the head waters of the rivers mentioned in the Garden of Eden. These rivers were later covered by the great flood in the days of Noah. After the flood, they retained their historic names. In the same way, certain place names will be retained in the Kingdom even though the topography has changed. Whether or not they will be in the exact locations is not stated, but they will be given as reference points, to show that God keeps His promises.

THE HEAVENLY CITY OF JERUSALEM

The Kingdom Age is unique because of its two major cities. The earthly city of Jerusalem that will be renamed "The LORD is there" in the Kingdom (see Ezekiel 48:35, NASV), has already been discussed. The second major city is the heavenly city of Jerusalem.

According to the writer of Hebrews, Abraham lived by faith ". . . as an àlien in the land of promise, as in a foreign *land*, dwelling in tents with Isaac and Jacob, fellow-heirs of the same promise; for he was looking for the city which has foundations, whose architect and builder is God" (Hebrews 11:9–10, NASV).

Abraham is called the "friend of God" (see Isaiah 41:8; 2 Chronicles 20:7). He was a man of faith. He trusted God to be his friend. God trusted Abraham to be His friend. As a friend, but also as His sovereign Lord, God kept all of His promises to Abraham. Fulfilling His promise to His friend Abraham, and to all who by faith become the children of Abraham, God has prepared a heavenly city to be their dwelling place.

John, in the Revelation, gives a description of the heavenly city of Jerusalem. He says:

> And I saw the holy city, new Jerusalem, coming down out of heaven from God, made ready as a bride adorned for her husband. And I heard a loud voice from the throne, saying, "Behold, the tabernacle of God is among men, and He shall dwell among them, and they shall be His peoples, and God Himself shall be among them, and He shall wipe away every tear from their eyes; and there shall no longer be any death; there shall no longer be any mourning, or crying, or pain; the first things have passed away" (Revelation 21:2–4, NASV).

At first glance it appears that this heavenly city of Jerusalem is the earthly city of Jerusalem, described by the prophet Ezekiel or Isaiah. Closer examination, however, reveals that this is not the case. They are two separate and distinct cities. This is clear in a description which John later gives of the heavenly city of Jerusalem. He states: "And the city is laid out as a square, and its length is as great as the width; and he measured the city with the rod, fifteen hundred miles; its length and width and height are equal" (Revelation 21:16, NASV). The earthly city of Jerusalem, as described by Ezekiel, is not anywhere near this large (see Ezekiel 48:35).

John continues his description of the heavenly city of Jerusalem saying, "And I saw no temple in it, for the Lord God, the Almighty, and the Lamb, are its temple" (Revelation 21:22,

NASV). During the Kingdom, the earthly city of Jerusalem is bordered by the great Temple to its north. Above and within the great Sanctuary, the Shekhinah presence of God dwells (see Ezekiel 43:1–9). However, there is no Temple in the heavenly city of Jerusalem. Instead, John is told that the Temple has been replaced by the Presence of God.

God's presence dwelling within the earthly Temple during the Kingdom Age, and His presence manifested in the heavenly city of Jerusalem, reveals the omnipresence and omnipotence of God. Because He is God, He can inhabit both cities.

Before His death, Jesus made a promise to His disciples, and to all who by faith trust Him to be their Lord and Savior. He said:

> *Let not your heart be troubled: believe in God, believe also in Me. In My Father's house are many dwelling places; if it were not so, I would have told you; for I go to prepare a place for you. And if I go and prepare a place for you, I will come again, and receive you to Myself; that where I am, there you may be also (John 14:1–3, NASV).*

Jesus told His disciples that He was going away, to prepare a dwelling place for all who believe in Him. The dwelling place being prepared is the heavenly city of Jerusalem. It is the place where all believers will dwell in their eternal, resurrected bodies. The heavenly city of Jerusalem memorializes God's total program of redemption and judgment among Israel and the nations.

Jesus emphasized that there are many dwelling places in His Father's house. The inference is to the omnipresence and omnipotence of God. The Psalmist expressed God's omnipresence. He penned:

> *Where can I go from Thy Spirit?*
> *Or where can I flee from Thy presence?*
> *If I ascend to heaven, Thou art there;*
> *If I make my bed in Sheol, behold, Thou art there.*

If I take the wings of the dawn,
If I dwell in the remotest part of the sea,
Even there Thy hand will lead me,
And Thy right hand will lay hold of me
(Psalm 139:7–10, NASV).

God's person and Presence dwelling in the heavenly city of Jerusalem in no way diminishes the fact of His person and Presence dwelling in His sanctuary on earth during the Kingdom. His presence within both cities confirms that He keeps His promises to all who have placed their trust in Him!

The heavenly city of Jerusalem will be the abode for resurrected Old Testament saints, for resurrected and raptured Church saints, for resurrected Tribulation saints (believers who died or who were martyred during the Tribulation), and for Kingdom saints (those born in the Kingdom) who may die during the Kingdom Age. The fact that its only occupants are the resurrected, raptured and redeemed saints is apparent from the words of John in the Revelation. He wrote: "and nothing unclean and no one who practices abomination and lying, shall ever come into it, but only those whose names are written in the Lamb's book of life" (Revelation 21:27, NASV).

This description does not fit the earthly city of Jerusalem, where sin-offerings will continue to be made. Neither does it fit the description of eternity, because in eternity all sinners will already have been judged. It does, however, fit into the Kingdom Age because death will still be a reality. Even in the Kingdom Age, death for the believer (those whose names have been written in the Lamb's book of life) will open the entrance into the heavenly city of Jerusalem.

Evidently, the heavenly city of Jerusalem also plays an important role in governing and administrating the earthly 1000 year Messianic Kingdom on the earth. Although it cannot be stated conclusively, it would appear that the heavenly city of Jerusalem is a great satellite city positioned over the earthly city of Jerusalem. The Scriptures indicate that the nations will walk in its light (see Revelation 21:23; Isaiah 4:5–6).

It would appear that the heavenly city of Jerusalem comes down out of heaven at the very beginning of the Kingdom Age, and will be visible to all residents of the earth. As it hovers over the earthly city of Jerusalem, its light and radiance will give visual evidence of God's Presence in heaven and on earth (see Revelation 21:9–11).

As the Kingdom progresses, however, it seems that the light of the heavenly city of Jerusalem will be diffused, as God causes a "unique day" to come upon the Kingdom (see Zechariah 14:7). With the heavenly city dimmed from view, children born during the Kingdom will be given an opportunity to accept, by faith, the existence of the heavenly Jerusalem and all that it promises. With Satan bound, and with lying and deception a thing of the past, none would question its existence. However, mankind will still have a sin nature, and God will give yet another opportunity for men and women, boys and girls, to exercise faith in Him. Sadly, Scripture indicates that there will be those who will choose not to believe.

When the 1000 years are ended, Satan will be released. In his last attempt to overthrow God, he will be victorious in deceiving many who are born in the Kingdom (see Revelation 20:7–10). However, Satan's victory will be short-lived, for God will immediately judge him and all those who follow him.

When the Messianic Kingdom comes to an end, and after all sin and sinners have been judged, God has promised to create a new heaven and a new earth. Moreover, the heavenly city of Jerusalem will continue to exist as an everlasting memorial to the promises of God and to His faithfulness to everyone who, by faith, will place their trust in Him.

God is a covenant-keeping God! His promises will never fail! God promised the nation of Israel a glorious future, and that promise is extended to anyone who will trust Him!

ADDITIONAL READING

CHOSEN PEOPLE MINISTRIES' PRODUCTS

Fuchs, Daniel, and Harold A. Sevener. *From Bondage to Freedom*. Neptune, N.J.: Loizeaux Brothers, 1995. Deals with the "400 silent years" between the close of the Old Testament and the opening of the New.

Sevener, Harold A. *Daniel: God's Man in Babylon*. Charlotte, N.C.: Chosen People Ministries, 1995. A comprehensive study of the Book of Daniel.

For a free copy of a catalog of books, tapes, and videos available through CHOSEN PEOPLE MINISTRIES, call 1-800-333-4936.

About
CHOSEN PEOPLE MINISTRIES, INC.

CHOSEN PEOPLE MINISTRIES, INC. (CPM) (formerly ABMJ-AMERICAN BOARD OF MISSIONS TO THE JEWS), was raised up by God to bring the Gospel to the Jewish people. It is an independent work supported by thousands of individual contributors and churches.

OUR MINISTRIES

It is our specific ministry to preach the Gospel of Yeshua, the Messiah, and to show our Lord's love to the Jewish people throughout the world. A direct and sustained witness is carried out by the following means:

- Establishing Messianic congregations.

- Holding fellowship meetings, Bible studies, worship services, and doing personal work. Each worker is trained and able to lead home discussion groups and provide home instruction for inquirers. We emphasize returning to the God of Israel through faith in the finished work of Yeshua haMashiach (Jesus the Messiah) for the forgiveness of sin so that one might enter into the spiritual blessings promised to the Jews. Our workers are also trained to present the relationship between the Old and New Covenants.

- Employing canvassing techniques. This work is done through telephone calls and personal door-to-door visits.

- Helping churches relate to the Jewish people and thereby increasing the witness to them. This is done through the following methods:

Monthly publishing of *The Chosen People* newsletter, a periodical for Christians with news of interest regarding Jews, our work among them, Jewish customs and traditions, and an interpretation of contemporary events. This informative and insightful magazine will keep you abreast of the world of Jewish missions and evangelism. You will be blessed as you read the testimonies of Jewish people who have accepted Yeshua as their Messiah and Savior.

Presentations explaining our work and special programs geared to inform Christians about the prophetic significance of some Jewish holidays, and so forth.

Distributing an extensive variety of books and tracts, as well as audio and video tapes.

Producing special radio and TV broadcasts designed to provide a witness to the Jewish community and to provide insight and instruction to Christians; our TV programs are most often aired during Jewish holidays.

Special ministry to children and young people. Each of our congregations has classes for small children and teenagers. Most have some kind of thrust toward college students. Each year our congregations conduct a camp for children and teenagers.

Volunteer programs for laypersons interested in direct involvement with CHOSEN PEOPLE MINISTRIES.

OUR BELIEFS

All workers and Board members of CHOSEN PEOPLE MINISTRIES must subscribe to doctrines fundamental to the faith. We declare and affirm our belief in the following:

- The Divine inspiration, infallibility, and authority of both the Old and New Covenants

- The Triune God and the Deity of the Lord Jesus (Yeshua) as the only begotten Son of God, and the promised Messiah

- His sacrificial blood atonement at Calvary, His bodily resurrection from the dead, and His premillennial second coming

- The necessity of presenting the Gospel to the Jewish people.

The present emphasis of CHOSEN PEOPLE MINISTRIES is on expanding the work among the Jewish people in large urban areas. CHOSEN PEOPLE MINISTRIES also continues active works in Israel, Canada, South America, Kiev and Germany, and is planning, by the grace of God, to establish effective outreaches in the 11 countries where 94% of the world's Jewish population will live by the year 2000.

As an arm of the local church to the Jewish community, CHOSEN PEOPLE MINISTRIES cannot function independently of the rest of the Body (the Church at large). We need your help. Paul reminds us that it is the responsibility of the Church to share the Gospel with Jewish people (Romans 1:16, 17).

How would you answer this question: "What have I done for the Jewish people, considering what they have done for me?" It was through the Jews that our Messiah, the Lord Jesus, came. It was through the Jews that our Scriptures were given. It is to the Jews that our Messiah will return (Zechariah 12:10). Shouldn't they have the same opportunity to hear the Gospel as the Gentiles? With your prayers and financial support, together we can reach the Jewish people.

OUR PROMISE TO YOU

As an organization dating from 1894, we can make you a promise that we have made and kept through over 100 years of ministry. We promise that your name and address will never be sold, traded, or given to any other organization or individual. Our mailing lists remain strictly confidential.

As a supporter of this ministry you will receive our monthly publication, *The Chosen People* newsletter. You will receive a monthly prayer letter stating our needs and giving you the opportunity to contribute to a particular worker or project. You will also receive a thank you letter and receipt for every gift you give. From time to time the missionaries whom you support through our organization will share personally with you and will send you praise and progress reports concerning their particular work, asking you to pray for specific needs.

As a Charter Member of the ECFA (the Evangelical Council for Financial Accountability), we are committed to having outside auditors publish our financial statements. In Canada we are members of the CCCC (Canadian for Christian Charities), the Canadian affiliate of the ECFA. Upon request you may receive a copy of their statement and full financial disclosure.